TulipTree review

Summer 2019 / issue #6

New Writers

ISBN: 978-0-9977944-8-9
Cañon City, Colorado
Publisher & Editor in Chief, Jennifer Top

www.tuliptreepub.com

Contents

[illegible]

Grand Prize Winner

Gingerbread House

Daniel Zeiders

INFERTILE. STERILE. BARREN. THIS WAS SOMETHING WE FOUND OUT AFTER marrying. A doctor said it just like that, *sterile*. He said it to my husband in a small office behind the examination rooms, both of us there for the results. After my own doctor visits and after my husband had told me everything was okay, I realized in that cramped office without a window that I should've been the supportive one, the one holding him, whispering into his ear.

He was sad in the quiet way. He began to get up earlier and go to bed later. I would check on him out in the living room, sitting alone watching late-night commercials, eyes glazed. I told him we could adopt, that this wasn't the end of possibilities. He knew that, he'd said, he just didn't want to talk about it right now. I didn't know what to do. After a while, when he got out of bed, I would slide over into his spot and go back to sleep, holding on to the dissipating warmth.

He began to bake sweets. My friends said he was trying to provide for me in other ways. Chocolate cupcakes and strawberry tarts. Gooey pecan pies. Cinnamon rolls. Rows of confections crowded our laminate countertops. When it snowed outside, he baked spice cakes and pumpkin pies. One day, I found him hovering over a tray of gingerbread figures.

"Smells good," I said.

"There is something off about them," he told me, and I saw a bite had been taken out of one of their legs. I plucked it up and bit down on the head. It was still soft and warm in the middle. I tasted molasses and brown sugar; he watched me chew.

"What do you think?"

"Delicious, though a little nude for my taste," I said and picked up the piping bag and iced a shirt onto the cookie. My husband added the gumdrops, and we worked side by side until they were all clothed and smiling.

He made gingerbread figures from then on, and I tried to help him or spend time near him as he mixed ingredients. We risked becoming the weird couple who made gingerbread for everyone, but he seemed happier because of it. He bought finer ingredients, expensive utensils. A professional oven replaced the stove that came with the house. I couldn't be with him for every batch, though I tried in the beginning. He was always mixing and cooking and writing down recipes. Eventually, I let him have his space downstairs, and I worked from my office above.

One day, he called me from the kitchen where he had a tray cooling on the counter. This cookie was much larger than the others; I wondered how he'd gotten it to fit in the oven. It looked undercooked, the air bubbles wiggling it around. Then I realized the cookie figure was trying to unstick itself from the cooking tray.

"I did it," my husband whispered.

It raised a doughy arm, and the thing gurgled sporadically until it cleared its throat with an earsplitting shriek. I backed away, but my husband got closer, hands unsure how to help. The thing tried to roll off the sheet and to its side, still screaming. I didn't know how it was making the noise. It rolled too far and landed face-down on the tile with a thick splat.

We could still hear a muffled note coming from it. I picked up the rolling pin from the counter and aimed for the head. My husband cried out in alarm. I smashed the head in half, but the thing still made sound. We both stood there, the energy of the moment stapled both of us immobile against our kitchen cabinets. The splattered cookie moved its appendages slowly like a grotesque squid. My husband scooped a handful of the head and took a bite. It looked monstrous, him kneeling in front of that brown mess and eating. But the thing grew quieter with every handful he swallowed. As soon as the last chunk of the head was off the floor, the kitchen was finally quiet. We looked at each other. He had smears on his chin and was breathing with his mouth open. I thought about how hot the gingerbread must've been. I got up and brought him the milk from the fridge. Still in shock, I slid down the wall and sat next to him as he drank from the jug.

"How did you know that would work?" I asked him.

He shook his head. "I didn't."

We sat there for a while listening to the sounds of the quiet house.

"I think I know how to fix it, though," he said.

I didn't ask him what that meant. The only worse thing than the answer in my head was his answer, floating invisibly in the space between us. I didn't stop him.

He upgraded the oven again; now restaurant-sized. He bought high-quality ingredients in bulk. My husband had a welder make an intricate set of cookie cutters he would keep in reach like surgeon's tools. I would hear the birthing screams from my office upstairs. They would always get quieter as my husband put them out of their misery by the mouthful. My husband gained weight. Extra pudge grew around his middle and his face became softer. I stayed upstairs; I hated to see him eat. I closed the door and pretended nothing was happening on the other side. Soon, though, the screams evolved into painful sobbing. The sobbing into agonized moaning. After endless cycles of suffering, what my calendar marked as months later, there was a soft knock on my door.

I opened the door, and my husband was there in the hall, smiling. Behind him was a four-foot figure: a gingerbread child. Sugar granules sparkled in its smooth brown skin. Its finer features frosted on, wide white eyes looking into mine searching for something. It seemed like an alien, awkwardly standing there and trembling slightly. I had to sit, and my husband joined me. He knelt and cried happily. The gingerbread child mirrored my action and sat down in the hallway, still curious.

My husband was a good father. They were inseparable. He narrated his entire day to the child while it followed him around like a duckling: I am putting on a shirt, I am pouring a glass of water, I am gathering up the trash. He taught the child words, and it learned them quickly. They walked around the house pointing at different things, giving them names. It pointed at me. Mommy, it called me in a voice soft and wispy.

We called it Cookie: an endearing name from my husband, an arms-length designation from me.

I wasn't a good mother, though I tried. I didn't feel any connection to it. When I turned around, it startled me. There it was. Like an ugly tattoo I had forgotten about but occasionally saw in the bathroom mirror. Its mouth always agape and eyes continually scanning the room. I didn't understand it at all. I tried to feed it, but it never seemed hungry. It never got dirty and if it did, how would we clean it? It didn't sleep, and I suspected it crept around the house at night. My world altered slightly every day, almost unnoticeable. Things moved around in every room, turned in odd angles. Its fingerprints seemed everywhere. I would drive to the coffee shop to try and occupy a space untouched by Cookie. This lasted until the baristas came up with a new specialty: gingerbread mochas.

When it learned every word in the house, it wanted to learn what was outside. My husband was entirely unaware of any strangeness about the whole thing. So, we took it for walks around the suburb, often to the small park at the center of the neighborhood.

ONLY A COUPLE WEEKS OLD and it was talking and saying hi to the playground children, mostly to their backs as they ran away from it. Full playgrounds and parks would slowly empty when we brought

Cookie. Once, it wanted to join a group kicking a soccer ball around, but the kids scattered as soon as Cookie approached. They'd left their ball and didn't come back for it. Cookie kicked the ball around with my husband until dark. I thought about getting it a dog to play with, but the other dogs in the suburb always tried to lick or take bites of it when they passed by on walks.

The other parents didn't like it, and I didn't blame them. It was different from their meat and bone kids. If they were brave, they would ask me, "Is that . . . yours?" Usually, they just stared at Cookie or at me. I hated it. Their eyes x-rayed me, looking for an obvious sign of a flaw.

Cookie liked to run. It was faster than my husband and didn't tire at all. My husband winded easily. We bought a frisbee. My husband would throw it, and Cookie would sprint after the disk and retrieve it. We timed it on our phones. I wrote down the numbers and showed Cookie the result each time.

"It's not 'fetch,'" my husband insisted.

Some of our walks ended up near the high-school track and this excited Cookie more than the frisbee. We stood outside the chain-link fence and watched the high school kids pass the baton to one another. Cookie followed the runners with its frosted eyes and laughed whenever anyone blew a whistle. We stayed until the practice was over, and everyone had gone.

One of the houses had an evening sprinkler water the lawn, one of those that fanned streams of water around. Cookie was curious and held out its hand under the passing stream. The water drizzled across it. I heard the sharp intake of breath and then a cry of surprise. It backed away from the sprinkler fast and held its hand out to my husband. The stream had made the gingerbread of the palm soft and a line of divots was now across it. We rushed home, and my husband used my hair dryer on the soggy wounds. The water hadn't gone through to the other side of the hand, but there were still noticeable scars.

It kept watching us for a reaction. I don't think it felt pain but was taking cues from both of us about how bad it was. At the dinner table instead of watching us eat, we watched it examine the wound. I wondered how brittle Cookie really was. How could it run without fracturing everything?

Cookie kept wanting us to take it to the school in the afternoon to watch the kids run around the track. It wanted to go out there and run too. My husband explained that they were not playing a game but practicing a sport. When the runners left the track and the evening orange colored the sky, we would let Cookie run a lap or two on its own. It would make shrill noises we decided were whistles while it ran.

"Should Cookie go to school?" my husband asked one night.

"I don't think they would let Cookie in," I answered truthfully.

"But I think Cookie needs other kids somehow," he said.

"But Cookie isn't a kid; it's a . . ."

"A cookie." My husband found what I had trouble saying. We lay there in silence. We heard Cookie explore the drawers in the bedroom upstairs.

"Our cookie," I said.

Weeks later, we ended up outside the school again, but instead of small groups of runners, tents and cars were lining the streets. Kids in different colored uniforms mingled about and stretched. The stands were half filled with groups of parents, cameras at the ready. Announcements blasted through the PA system.

"A track meet," my husband explained to Cookie.

We didn't need to buy tickets to sit in the stands, and we watched groups of sprinters take off with every blast of an air horn. Cookie seemed to like this better than the whistle and tried to hoot along with it. The parents around us stared. I felt embarrassed by their looks and asked Cookie to watch quietly. Cookie seemed put out. I realized what I had done, that I had given in to these judgmental strangers and let them dictate how we would act. I got angry but quickly put the fire out. At the next air-horn blast I hooted along with it, and Cookie smiled. All three of us hooted like owls for the next couple of races. A man in front of us moved down the stands, away from our parliament. I felt a rush of rude glee.

We watched the races get longer, sometimes punctuated by the discus throwers in the middle of the field. There was a nice order to everything, and from our vantage, it looked like one of those complicated pictures you see in a search-and-find children's book.

I heard a woman ask another if she should go get her umbrella from her car. I looked up. Dark gray clouds were overhead, ready to open upon us. I told my husband we should go. He stopped watching the runners like I had shaken him out of a daze. We both looked at the empty spot to his right. Cookie had gone.

We both rushed down the stands to the barrier between the stands and the track, looking for our small, brown cookie-child. My husband pointed to the line of staggered runners in their starting positions. Cookie was hiding next to them, off the side of the track but ready to run. The horn blew, and all the runners took off, including Cookie, who merged onto the track with them.

The first runners didn't realize there was an extra competitor, but a couple of the ones waiting for a baton did and didn't move when their teammates got there, only pointing and looking at their coaches for orders. Some parents from the stands were booing, and a coach was furiously blowing his whistle, jogging through the field in the middle of the track. I felt drops of rain on my face during the second baton pass. My husband hopped the fence.

Only two lanes were running at the third baton pass, and Cookie caught up to them. Everyone seemed to have stopped to watch. My husband was making about as much progress as the coach, which was very little. Water droplets now covered the lens of my glasses, and I took them off. I distinctly heard a voice behind me: "What is that thing?"

Cookie was still running, but I could tell the rain was making its body heavier. It pumped its arms to keep up with the last runner, and as they came around the final bend, one of Cookie's arms flung off onto the track. It didn't seem to notice.

I don't know what the lead runner expected when he glanced behind him, checking to see how much of a lead he'd gotten, but he wasn't expecting Cookie. He stumbled to the side, into the next lane over and stopped, in shock. Cookie made it across the finish line and crumpled to the ground, one foot twisted weirdly and the rain now coming down steadily. My husband was the first one to get to Cookie, but a group quickly formed around them. I clambered over the short chain-link fence and pushed through the small crowd.

My husband cradled it on the track. Cookie looked bad. Someone held an umbrella over us, but the wet cookie flesh was already softening into slushy mud. The frosted features of the face splotched and smeared together, the eyes looking to my husband. It saw my husband in distress and started to cry out to him. It was different from the cries of pain I'd heard from the other cookies. Louder and panicked. Cookie's deformed torso jerked violently, and the frosting streaks trickled across my husband's arms and puddled onto the ground. The scream grew louder. To the horror of those gathered around, my husband lifted Cookie's warped head and bit down. The howl quieted a little.

I huddled onto the track next to him and put an arm around my husband's shoulders. A person on the edge of the circle was getting sick, but everyone else was silent. My husband chewed and cried quietly. I scooped some of our cookie child into my mouth. Ginger. Nutmeg. Cinnamon.

Fat Bitch

Ry Molloy

GRANNY STILL LIVED IN HER HOUSE BY THE BAY. IT WAS A CUTE PLACE, ONE story with a wraparound patio, where she spent her days in a brown wicker rocking chair, sipping a glass of red zinfandel and staring down the street toward the ocean. If you sat still, you could hear the waves from there, beneath the slurring clang of her rusty wind chimes and the creak of the home's shoddy woodwork. It was not particularly nice, the house. I think Granny sacrificed luxury for closeness to the water, but the place felt idyllic. It made me think of a simpler time, when the world was smaller, when people lived their whole lives in one town and knew each of their neighbors by name. Despite this, I had not paid a visit in years. Going there reminded me how much I hated my grandmother. I mean, in some way, I loved her—in the way that I had no choice but to love her—but I could only summon this goodwill by reminding myself that soon she would die.

It was December when my father called to inform me that she had been snowed in, to which I suggested he get his son for the job, which led him to tell me that I would regret it if I didn't help, you fat bitch, he added. Years ago, he would throw things when I disobeyed—shoes, chairs, full cans of light beer—not at me but rather at the walls against which I cowered, enough to scare me into compliance. He was not a violent man, but he frustrated easily. Now that I no longer lived with him, he used guilt. So, I drove to my grandmother's house out of guilt, yes, and to prove that, as someone capable of feeling guilt, I was not in fact a fat bitch.

There was something else as well. A couple weeks prior, Grandpa had passed. That was the first time I had seen Granny in years, at the funeral. Throughout my childhood, she had expressed little apart from remarks on my weight. She seemed more emotionless stone than woman, and I had assumed she was incapable of love. She had the pained smile of someone being stuck with a long needle, and she was always barking at everyone. I imagine that was why my father never stood up to her, because her wrath was so loud and so ruthless. But at Grandpa's funeral, the woman I saw was not scary. She was broken, folded over Grandpa's body, sobbing and shaking. When they lowered the casket into the ground, she screeched like a wounded dolphin. I had never heard anyone cry like that before, and I suppose this was also why I went to her house, because I wanted a piece of it. I drove there that day with the tiniest glint of hope, a candle set out in a blizzard, that I would make a pleasant memory with my grandmother before she died the death I had long awaited.

The drive was only an hour, a straight shot down the interstate. When I was a child, and we visited each week, the trip felt like an eternity, an endless stretch of pine forest, two-lane highway, and the occasional lake. As I got older, though, the trips took on a new sort of excruciating slowness. I remember sitting in the backseat, clutching my legs to my chest, wondering which part of my body she would mention: my stomach spilling over the rim of my hips, my bulky nine-year-old calves, my porcine cheeks. She spoke of me as though I were not old enough to feel bad about myself, and the rides back home were hardly better, cramped in a cold sedan, my mother shouting at my father that he can't let that woman talk about me like that, my little brother giggling, and my father tightening his grip on the steering wheel, replying that someone had to get the message across.

It was true. I needed to lose weight, though my father seemed to think I did not know this. He was always giving me chores that made little sense and required frequent bending of the back and knees. In the fall, he would make me gather all the pine cones from the yard and stack them behind the shed. In the spring, he would hand me gloves and instruct me to rid the lawn of crabgrass and dandelions. To this day, he claims these were innocent requests, but I know that he was trying to teach me a lesson. The lesson was that I was fat. If my body hurt enough—or so went his logic—I would learn this lesson and begin to heal. He was cut from the same cloth as my grandmother, who preferred a more blunt method of instruction.

When I was six, she told me that if I kept eating the caramels from the bowl on her coffee table, I would grow so big that I would explode, like the blueberry girl from that movie. At age ten, she began planting herself by the dessert table at family functions, waiting for me to approach so she could wave her finger at me as though I were a dog attempting to have some people food. Even at eighteen, by which time I weighed two hundred pounds, she persisted, telling me that no man would ever love me if he could not lift me over the threshold. This she did not say to me but rather to the room at large, as we sat in her den eating crackers and cheddar cheese cubes. My mother was the only one who ever spoke back to her, but she was hardly around anymore. Both my father and brother looked down at their laps. Alone, I ran out to the porch and cried.

I PARKED IN FRONT of Granny's and noticed the snow over her home was untouched. Her Toyota sat in the driveway, buried up to its tires. There were no lights on inside and no footprints from the door, so I assumed she was asleep. Like a small, hermetic rodent, Granny rarely ventured outside in the wintertime. The cold icy ground was no place for old women. On the news, I had heard about these sisters from a few towns over. Both widowed and in their late eighties, they moved into a home together. One night, after returning from the movie theater, the older one stepped out of the car and slipped on a patch of ice. Her sister raced around the car to lift her up, and, in doing so, she fell as well. It was a Sunday night in a quiet neighborhood, and no one who drove by noticed them there at the end of their driveway. Nobody heard whatever sounds called out from their mouths, and it was not until the next day that a neighbor found them there, clutching each other, eyes frozen open.

I grabbed my shovel and dug in at the end of Granny's driveway, where the snow was heavier, having been compacted by the passing plows. By the time I'd cleared that area, I was panting. I fished a protein bar from my pocket and ate it. I stabbed the shovel into the snow and lay down for a moment. Although the temperature was somewhere in the twenties, sweat ran slick down my forehead and back. I was cooking inside my snow gear, like a sausage in a bun. When I unzipped my jacket to breathe, I could smell my body odor wafting out from my layers. My thighs ached, and my arms were starting to give out, but then I remembered how much I hated my grandmother, how much joy it would bring her to know that I was too weak for the job. On this wave of pure, unadulterated spite, I continued.

By noon, I had finished the driveway and was on to scraping the ice from her front steps. I contemplated leaving a few slabs in place, just to see what might happen, but once again, guilt pulled me in a different direction. Inside, I found nobody home and assumed that she was out playing cards. I removed my wet gear and sat in her armchair. It had mahogany claw feet, and when I shifted my weight, some of her scent eeked out of its pink velour upholstery: stale grapes and moth balls. I got up and grabbed a bottle of whiskey from her cabinet, poured a glass, and sat back down. When I finished it, I poured another.

A year ago, I had stopped drinking, but as I waited in the cool musty air of Granny's house, I was gripped by a desire to take something that belonged to her. I was never an alcoholic or anything like that. The problem was that on more than one occasion, I had drunk too much, blacked out, and, while in the murky between of my waking unconsciousness, committed an act of rage. My therapist claimed these outbursts were the result of alcohol being used to repress anger, but this did not make sense to me. I did not drink because I was angry. I drank because I was out with my friends who were also drinking, because I knew that I was boring, and I wanted to be exciting. Often, it worked. I would take a couple shots, tell cruel jokes about my weight, and hit it off with strangers. Sometimes, I even danced with them or took them home. When it did not work, however, the results were disastrous. One second, I would be on the dance floor, hands in the air, shaking my ass, and the next thing I'd know, my friends were surrounding me, gripping me under their arms, and dragging me out of the bar.

Where are we going? I'd slur.

Annie, you just punched that dude in the face.

As I worked my way through glass number two, not only was I nowhere near blacking out, but I also felt a serenity in that chair. I was buzzed enough to ignore the years of insults that had been spewed from where I currently sat. I took deep breaths, settling down from all of the shoveling. Slowly, the blood seeped back into my extremities. This was once the seat of evil, I imagined myself telling my future husband, an entity for whom I often prepared mentally. I would have much to tell him about this chair when we one day had a home together.

I poured another glass and walked about the house, planning which other objects I would claim when Granny died. First, there was the chair, which, no matter how old and tattered it became, I would take for symbolic purposes, like a knight who keeps the tooth of a dragon he's slain. Elsewhere in the den, I staked claim over the grandfather clock. I also decided I would have her tacky green area rug, if only to burn it, and her crystal decanter, if only to smash it. I walked over to her fridge, inside of which was half of a Boston cream donut, several heads of garlic, and two jugs of zinfandel that sat on the part of the door where one normally keeps milk. I closed the fridge and checked the freezer, which was stocked with frozen meals. I pulled out one labeled Asian Chicken, opened it, and tossed the tray into the microwave. When it finished, I pulled it out, took one bite, and threw the rest into the trash. It was one o'clock now. I wanted to leave but knew Granny would never thank me if I did. She was the type of woman who expected things. She thought that the world—and everyone in it—owed her something. Should she arrive home to a fully shoveled driveway and porch, it was all just as well. She would make no effort to track down the doer of the deed; rather, she would walk inside with the assurance that she'd been blessed with what she deserved.

I perused her bedroom next, deciding that her linens were too dingy for me to inherit, and the large mirror above her headboard was stained with decades of dust. It also made my face look wider. A framed photo caught my eye on the nightstand. At first, I thought it was a photo of my brother, Luke—that narrow hooked nose and front teeth big as tombstones—but I looked again and realized it was my father, albeit a young, grinning, puppy-eyed version. My first instinct, of course, was to pick it up and throw it at the wall, which I did. It didn't break, though, and when I picked it up and stared at it, I grew disgusted with their shared resemblance, in which I saw nothing of myself.

My brother was two years younger than me, and even though we were the same height, he had weighed almost a hundred pounds less than me for as long as I could remember. Sometimes I felt like the practice child, that by growing up witnessing what I endured for my weight, my brother had learned the right way to be. It would not be fair to call my brother and me polar opposites, but it felt as though each direction I had taken in life, he had taken another. Growing up, I had few hobbies. I was not good at anything other than baking—that and watching fantasy movies in my bedroom. Luke, however, excelled at everything he tried. Our father put him in soccer leagues, signed him up for acting classes, sent him to camps that molded young men into leaders of tomorrow. We went to the same high school, and everyone loved him. Teachers often remarked, upon seeing my last name on their roll call, that they did not know Luke had a sister. Then they would look at me closely for a moment, almost wincing, and then move on, as though they had tried to spot an ounce of Luke's greatness in me and came up empty-handed. It never felt as though Luke were ashamed of me, but the rest of the world was embarrassed enough. In the end, I turned out fine. I went to a college in state. I became a nurse, paid off my debt, and now lived in a mill condominium just north of the city. To me, this felt good enough. Luke, however, was more adventurous. He had no plan for life and seemed unbothered by this. After studying performance art at a pricey college in California, he took a job teaching English in Korea. After that, he worked at Disney World, and from there he landed his first in what became a series of roles in ensemble casts aboard cruise liners. Once a year, he came home for a visit.

The thing about Luke is that he's disgustingly charming. He would burst through the front door, as though it were a curtain call, and scoop the both of us into bear hugs. He was muscular, and like a particularly virulent strain of disease, he only grew stronger with each passing year. And he could talk. He asked endless questions—my father's arthritis, my attempts at dating—and when through pretending to be interested in our tiny lives, he would share stories of his own. Meeting such and such diplomat at a gala in the Azores, climbing a mountain that was actually a volcano, getting stranded in Barbados for a week after missing his departure. Conveniently, in each of his trips home, though, there was never enough time for him to drive down to see Granny, who no doubt still worshipped him as well.

I FLUNG OPEN HER closet, knowing fully that I would not fit into her clothing. Still, there were some things that I wanted: two Coach purses, some silk scarves, an ivory Chanel suit that I would wear with intent to rip. I returned to the den with the photo of my father. With the whiskey gone, I rummaged through the cabinets and found an old bottle of rosé that I had bought for her years back while backpacking through western Europe. I had gone on the trip shortly after accepting my job at the hospital. With the rest of my life potentially sealed after accepting the position, it seemed like the right time to travel and find myself, as Luke would say. Quickly, I learned there was nothing to find. In each city, I stepped off the train, hopeful that something would call to me—the culture, the lifestyle—but nothing ever did. I waited in the lines and paid for the museums, but I had little interest in art or history. All of the famous squares and sculptures were crammed with sweaty tourists, and I was one of them. The hostels were horrible, sharing bathrooms with smelly Italian men and bunks with noisy German girls.

After two weeks of travel, I broke down in Paris. I booked an expensive hotel room where I holed up for three days, living off room service and binge watching the American channels with the blackout curtains pulled shut. I canceled my return flight—which was to come in two weeks—and flew home the next day. The only time I left the hotel room was to splurge on souvenirs. Some cured meats for my father, a jersey for Luke, and the wine for Granny.

The bottle had been opened, but barely any was missing. Clearly she had tried a sip and was disgusted, not caring that I had blown forty euros on it. By now it had gone bad. The delicate pink I remembered had turned to a viscous orange, and I took swig after swig, ignoring the thick sour taste. Nothing would ever please that woman, I realized, at least not anything from me. Desperate and drunk now, I paced around the house, trying to think of a reason to love her and finding nothing. I grabbed a broom and began sweeping, after that, a rag and spray. If there was no way to please her, the least I could do was clean. If I could not feel love for her, I would go through the motions until I did. The windows were cloudy, the floor stained and scratched, the furniture saturated with dust. I cleaned until I needed more to drink, and then I grabbed one of her zinfandel jugs from the fridge and started with that. It was hardly better than the rosé, acidic and sticky. I hoped it would lull me to sleep, but it only made me dizzy.

I walked over to my purse, grabbed a couple protein bars, and ate them in two bites apiece. I turned on the ceiling fan, drank another glass, and sat back down, staring at the photo on the coffee table. This was a mistake. I began to picture my father's face at Granny's eventual funeral, his disappointment and resentment for me etched in the lines of his brow, fully transferred from Granny's corpse to him. I imagined all of the ways he would think of to insult me and my body, and I imagined myself repeating them as he eulogized: spare tire, cellulite, lard. My stomach churned. I pictured my body swelling until it enveloped the room, my father, my brother, my unborn children, all suffocating beneath the weight of my unrestrained girth. I pictured myself laughing and laughing as all of them died around me. And then I was alone.

Just as I considered hopping in my car and driving it into the bay, the front door opened, and Granny called out, "Hello?"

I stood. "Granny, hello! It's Annie." I was very drunk. Awaiting her response, I noticed my arms were outstretched for a hug, and I lowered them.

"Is Dad here?" she asked, unfazed by both me and the fact that I had removed a metric ton of snow from her property. She was smothered—puffy gray jacket that went down to her calves, knitted scarf around her chin, big pink hat, and boots that swallowed her tiny legs. She looked like a child, bundled up to go play in the snow.

"Where's Dad?" she asked, sniffling and unfurling her scarf. That smell of stale grapes wafted into the air, and I remembered how I really felt about this woman.

"He didn't want to come," I said.

Nodding, she slid off her gloves and let them drop to the floor. She hung up her hat, and I saw that she still drew on her eyebrows, two auburn streaks over pale sickly skin. Her hair was that translucent color of dishwater brown, the result of follicles that can no longer hold pigment.

"Did you see the driveway?" I asked, and immediately I felt myself shrinking into my adolescence, into the sad little fat girl who tried to please her grandmother, the girl who would tug two fingers at the waistband of her jeans and exclaim with pride at the gap she had revealed, as though it were a card trick rather than the result of periodic starvation and compulsive crash diets—swearing off solid foods after one p.m., taming hunger with cotton balls dipped in sugar-free punch—the progress from which never lasting for long.

"Is Lucas around?" she asked. "My grandson?"

"Yes," I said without thinking.

"Very good," she said.

I stood there as she stepped out of her boots and walked to her chair. Then I sat on the adjacent couch. At first I was unsure as to why I'd said that Luke was coming, but as the thought settled over the room, I grew pleased with myself. That was when I realized that I did not actually want Granny to die; I simply wanted to hurt her. Perhaps, somewhere in me, I felt that keeping her company—upon Luke's inevitable failure to return—would cause her allegiance to shift, which when I really thought about it, was probably the whole reason I went after all, to prove to Granny that I was better than my brother. Granny reached for my half-empty glass of wine and sipped it as though it were hers. She let her head sink back into her chair, and she swirled her wrist. Then she said to me, impersonally as one might speak of the weather, "You're so large."

"Well," I replied, grinding my teeth, waiting to slip to that dark drunken place, where no morals existed, and there was nothing to stop me from tossing her down the basement steps. But my mind stayed put, and I kept talking. "My boyfriend has yet to complain," I said, which I thought was as good of a lie as my first.

"Really?" she said. "Where did you meet this boyfriend?"

"France," I said.

"France?" she asked.

"On the east side of Paris," I added. The words would not stop, and I could feel myself sweating. I did not know if there was an east side of Paris. Of course there was an eastern part, but they probably called it something more elegant. She seemed to believe it though, and a lie only need be sustained for the length of a life, which, in her case, would hopefully not be so long.

"Do you see him a lot?" she asked. "Your boyfriend?"

"Very often," I replied.

She cleared her sinuses and gulped, rapping her fist on her chest to help the wine along. Her breathing was belabored and scratchy, more like wheezing. For as long as I could remember, she'd had horrible COPD, but she refused to carry an oxygen tank. She was at the age where it was impossible to perform a single function without emitting grotesque noises. Her fingers cracked each time she clenched them, and her mouth made this gluey sound each time she opened it, like a boot being pulled from the mud.

"So, where did Lucas run off to?" she asked. She was getting impatient, but I knew that she would wait for as long as it took. Really, she had nothing she needed to make time for. She liked to watch the Patriots play, but my father had taught her how to record them, so the game times no longer had imminence. All she could do was sit and wait for visits from the family, but a part of me wondered if she even enjoyed them. Here I was, her only granddaughter, sitting across from her with a glass of wine, and she could hardly force a conversation.

"Come to think of it," I said, "He might have decided to leave."

"Nonsense." She brought her glass to her lips and slurped what was left of her wine. When she put down her glass, I refilled it.

"Your father didn't tell me you two were coming," she said. "I was out playing bridge."

"Well I'm here," I said.

She nodded then coughed and then cleared out her sinuses.

"Would you like something to eat?" I asked, not knowing what to say.

"No," she said. "But there's a donut in the fridge. I think Lucas would like it. That boy has such a good appetite."

I returned from the fridge with the plastic-wrapped donut and plopped it on the coffee table. Granny sat up at attention. Delicately, she unwrapped the donut, folded some napkins, and placed it on top of them. She turned it so the whole side was facing the door, and then she sat back in her chair, ready for him to arrive. We sat there for a bit, the ceiling fan churning and whipping up dust through the house. The napkins billowed beneath the donut, and I contemplated my next lie. Perhaps I would tell her that Lucas was gay, but instead I kept my mouth shut.

In spite of his abandonment, there was one thing about my brother that I loved. He was the first and, for all I knew, the only person who did not mind my weight. Sure, he made fun of me sometimes. When we got into fights, he would call me a fatso or lift up the back of my shirt to expose my muffin top, but deep down, I knew that he did not care. Despite how distant we had become, I believed that he loved me. When we were in high school, and our parents would take up the first floor with one their raucous arguments, he and I would retreat to the basement and roll a joint. He said that weed made him paranoid and that I was the only person he could smoke it around. We'd take turns filling our lungs and then blowing our smoke out in rings, something I was actually better at than him. We hardly said much on those nights. We just watched old cartoons, and occasionally, I would glance at him. He really was such a cute kid. So self-conscious, but you could only see it when no one was looking. He would offer to go make us food when the munchies kicked in, never anything fancy—chips and shredded cheese cooked in the microwave or a bowl of chocolate chip cookie dough—but when my parents would pause their fights and ask, he would claim that the food was his, not mine.

One night, as the divorce grew more imminent, which we could tell by the decreased frequency and volume of their fights, we got into a spat of our own. Lucas blamed our father for their marital problems, that he was an asshole to everyone aside from him and that our mother was right to leave him. I shouted back that our mom was selfish for wanting to leave him, which to this day I believe to be true. He sat up on his sofa and told me that he wanted to run away too, that he hated this house and everyone in it. I walked over to him and socked him in the jaw.

You're a fucking pussy, I shouted at him. That's why you want to leave. Because you're a little fucking pussy, and you have no idea what it means to be loyal. He lay there for a while, holding his jaw and seething, and only when I stopped yelling did he cry.

For the next couple years, we stopped talking, something that I learned was effortless to do but almost impossible to stop doing. Luke got accepted into his school, and my father agreed to pay for it. I was finishing up my nursing degree and still living at home then. One morning, as we prepared to drive Luke to the airport, I heard the muffled sound of retching coming from the bathroom. When the toilet flushed, I opened the door, and there he stood, glossy-eyed, wiping the grip of his toothbrush with toilet paper. What are you doing? I asked him. Leaving, he said, and as he took a step around me, I pinned him in the doorway and smacked him across the face. Where do you think you're going? I said, inches from his face. I don't know, he said. Let me go. And then he cried. Years later, I still didn't know what came over me. I still felt that nobody would ever love me as much as he did, and that if I were lucky, I would find someone who could even be bothered to hate me, and I would live out the rest of my life knowing at least I was noticed.

AT MY SUGGESTION, Granny and I moved out to the porch where we waited for Luke. I held her hand and led her to her rocking chair where I propped up her head with a pillow. This was the care that came naturally, the kind I afforded to any of my patients, the kind that years of nursing had hardwired into my brain. I offered blankets, checked their vitals, brought them water and whatever else they asked for. When they asked questions I could not answer—Am I going to make it?—I told them the doctor would be there soon.

The air outside was crisp and cold, still as the scene in a snow globe. A gust of wind blew snow from the ground to the air. The two of us sat on that porch until it was dark. We said hardly a word, pointing at the occasional rabbit poking out from a bank of snow and listening to the hiss of a wave breaking through the distant frozen shore. As stupid as it sounds, I began to actually think that Luke might show up. I did not want to hurt him; I just wanted to hold him. When Granny began to shiver, I fetched a quilt from inside and laid it over her. She looked at me with her frail hollow face, and I sensed there was something she wanted to say. It scared me, the anticipation of her words, but I waited, as always, as I would until the day she died, for some wall to break open and love to pour forth in any form. It never did. But on that day, when I looked at her, at the waning sun reflected in her eyes, I wanted her to be comfortable.

"Is Lucas all right?" she eventually asked.

"He'll be here soon," I replied.

Reflections on the First Barter

Alexander Abbas Kayhani

When I was in kindergarten
a flock of white pigeons flew above
the pool, surrounded by little blades of grass,
in the backyard.
Baba did his best
to make sure I had good friends
growing up.
He built an above-ground pool
and invited the neighborhood kids
into our home.

Their pale skin became red in the sun.
We splashed, laughed, jumped, kerplunked,
dunked, floated, loud joy above,
muffled joy submerged,
playing deeply in the cool gushing liquid,
and when the sun shone through it,
it was an amber wave.
"Baba!" I called out, "Hey, Baba, do we have any fudgesicles?"
He had bought them for all the kids.

"What's a 'Baba'?"
Confused countenances on all the little boys not yet friends—
All looking at me—
From far over there—
And I'm way over here—
To pull divergent tectonic plates back together.
"It's like 'dad,'" I said.
"Weird. Why didn't you just say that?"
Profile edges and horizons and turned away backs—
And slow awkward underwater walks away—
Away from me—

"Dad!" he didn't recognize, "Hey, Dad!" nothing.
Look at what I'm saying
Everyone . . .
"Dad!" he turned and the way his eyes looked at me . . .
"Who are you talking to?" he said,
"I'm not your 'Dad,' I am your 'Baba,'"
he said in front of Everyone,
"I do all this for you and you call me Dad?"
Hands stretch forward millennia
to put dirt on my head.*
But unsure why,
back then.
He turned
away from me . . .
His back—
and Baba walked into the house he bought with Mom
to celebrate
when they found out
I would be born.

Mom told me to apologize.
I climbed out, my body still soaked
from the pool.
I looked back at the blue swells of that mass of liquid,
and all the kids immersed
in the synthesis of countless flickering drops,
like the reification of a dense mirage;
and I was coated in the fluid—
get it off—
I reached for a towel—
But there were none.
The pigeons flew overhead again
A body in between them and the earth
And I was drenched.

Socks

Anne Katata

GRANDPA JAUME NEVER REALLY LIKED ANIMALS. AND HE ESPECIALLY DIDN'T LIKE them inside the house. Like a lot of folks, he felt that animals belonged outside in the yard, or the barn, anyplace that wasn't where you ate and slept. And this went for "pets," be they small dogs or cats. Actually he really didn't believe in the concept of pets. Animals were supposed to work for their keep. So, he was a little annoyed when we got Socks.

Socks wasn't always our cat. She was a smallish black and white cat with one blind eye who lurked around the field next to our house. Not sure what she lived off of, since we and the neighbors never fed her. Oftentimes we'd find her timidly waiting in the bushes near the drive leading to our gates. My dad likes to say that we were heavily arm-twisted at gun point to take her in. He blames that crazy American friend, the one with eleven cats back home, for us ending up with Socks. We were driving home from El Prat airport with la loca Americana when she saw Socks sitting outside our gate.

"Oh, whose cat is that? So cute."

Hoping to nip things in the bud, my parents in unison replied: "DO NOT FEED THE CAT! She's a stray. She's no one's cat. And she's not allowed in the yard. Got it?"

Brother Sergi, however, deflated their attack when he calmly added, "But we call her Socks."

"You named a stray cat you ignore and don't feed after President Clinton's cat?" came the incredulous reply. "Well, she's gonna get fed now. No cat named after Clinton's cat goes hungry on my watch."

Dad glared at Sergi in the rear-view mirror. "Okay, but feed her outside our gate!"

So, the crazy American lady fed Socks, outside our walls. Leftovers and scraps were cut up along with rice or gravy-soaked bread and left in a bowl near those bushes by the drive. And when she returned home two months later to her eleven cats, she left several bags of cat food in our cupboard. When the weather got cold and rainy, Socks was brought inside the gate and fed under the carport near the back door. The excuse given was that it was easier and no one got wet. Still my dad wasn't too happy, and Mom wondered how she'd explain the cat to Grandpa Jaume. But Sergi seemed pleased to have a cat in the yard who watched him practice his soccer moves.

One spring break Dad, Mom, and Sergi had to drive down to Andalucia for some soccer conference. Since my school was on a different schedule, Grandpa Jaume and Grandma Antonia came to stay with me in the house and to make sure I brushed my teeth and took regular showers. Since it was obvious that Grandpa wanted nothing to do with her, I had to feed Socks—it was usually Sergi's job. That was fine because Grandpa could help me with my homework instead.

Socks was usually pretty friendly with people, her short, crooked tail always up like a furry greeting. But she learned to stay away from Grandpa. She had a tendency to "get underfoot," trying to rub against our legs even when we were walking. Grandpa didn't seem to understand this, and oftentimes ended up kicking poor Socks, although I don't think he meant to hurt her. Anyway, she avoided him.

Socks had had a small litter of three kittens that spring, and when Grandpa and Grandma came to babysit me the little balls of fur were about eight weeks old but could easily fit in my cupped hands. One morning, while Grandpa was taking his coffee on the second-floor terrace, Socks started crying frantically, mewing the loudest I'd ever heard, screaming even. It sounded like someone was killing her.

Looking out my bedroom window I could see her pacing frantically around the soccer net in the yard. So, I called Grandpa that he had to come downstairs and see what all the fuss was about.

One of Socks's kittens—the one we called Barni after the Barcelona mascot—had somehow gotten himself all tied up in the soccer goal netting. And the more he struggled and tried to pull away, the tighter the netting wound around his little neck. By the time Grandpa came down and out to the garden, little Barni was gasping for air—he was being strangled. Try as he may, Grandpa just could not untie the mess tightening around him. So, he went inside, got Mom's sewing scissors, and cut the net.

"Dad's not going to like that at all," I said, looking at the hole and watching Barni run to his mom.

Socks was licking Barni furiously, trying to calm him down until he started purring. But once she soothed her baby, Socks walked over to Grandpa Jaume and started rubbing against his legs, letting out the biggest purr I ever heard. And meowing, as if saying thank you. I was afraid Grandpa would kick her away, but he just stood there, looking down at the little black and white cat at his feet, rubbing rubbing rubbing away at his trousers and leaving her hair on his shins. And then he bent down and patted her! Boy, you should've heard her purr then! I was even more surprised when Grandpa phoned Dad and Mom that night and told them what had happened.

"She thanked me! She thanked me! I didn't know a cat could do that!" he excitedly yelled into the phone. That exclamation was then followed by some silence and then his quiet response: "Oh, I had to cut it. Sorry."

During his last few months, Grandpa Jaume and Grandma Antonia came to live with us because they couldn't take care of themselves. On the day that Grandpa died, Socks got into the house and made a beeline for his room. Mom tried to get her out, but Grandpa said to leave her be. He died that evening with her on his bed, curled up by his side, one of his hands near her head. Once he had passed, she sniffed him, took a long last look, and then slowly walked back outside, tail down. Sergi said she was mourning.

Socks passed away this past autumn. She was close to twelve, not bad for a cat who spent her first few years scavenging and surviving in the fields until we took her in. Mom found her curled up under the fig tree. She'd thought she was sleeping until her hand met a cold stiff body. At least little Socks went peacefully. We buried her in the pine forest behind the house. Meanwhile Barni was adopted by Auntie Nuria, and his siblings found homes with some of Mom's university colleagues.

Dad never repaired the soccer net. Mom wouldn't let him. She said that the hole was there for a reason. Every time Sergi kicked a goal, the ball would somehow find the hole and sail on through it out the other side, sometimes landing in the pool. Sergi kicked a lot of goals—he was turning into our in-house Messi. Anyway, Mom said that at those times she was reminded of Grandpa Jaume and Socks.

Dedicated to the Tulloch-Jimenez family
of Vilanova i la Geltru, Spain,
and to the cats who have touched our lives.

Old Ladies Who Love to Swim

Dawn Marie Martin

They are the uninhibited, the not shy
and the first to arrive
clothed in their outdated stiff polyester bathing suits,
brown and orange towels draped around their necks.

They hobble gingerly down uneven ground towards the glassy lake water,
bodies wounded by time,
Helen has lost a breast to cancer
Anita has had both knees replaced, and trouble with her hip.

Into the cool dark water they dive with unexpected grace,
seconds pass.

They emerge out of nature's pool,
hair smooth as the water drains from the tips.
Droplets of water, like diamonds, sparkle on their skin.

As if some magical transformation has occurred,
they glide freely through the water,
Like fairies flying through air.

The small lake, whose edges are framed by tall evergreen trees, makes the ladies feel like they are fourteen again, diving in for the first time.

Giggling and following each other, they explore the many coves and corners the lake has to offer.
They sit for a while atop the immersed log at the end of the lake.

When they swim it's like their secret world opens up.
Gone are the years of worry, raising families and old age.
Their spirits soar, like the resident eagle circling the lake.

Truly, what a sight to behold, these two old ladies, who love to swim.

Stalker

Carter Keeling

Clouds of startled wonder
swam across his tired eyes
when he saw the ruins before him.

They were broken, sagging,
crumbled into tiny bits,
but held somehow
something deep inside;
he could've sworn he heard it
slowly, softly breathing.

The way to get in
snaked around a field of grass,
through a minefield and a river
filled with moss and crude oil.
He had stopped to take a nap,
already feeling weighed
by the building's growing energy.

He woke before too long,
after splashing his reflection
from the river in a dream.
He stood back up and walked,
hardly giving himself a moment to think.

The path to get inside
was clear to him now,
having traveled there
so many times before.
He traced along the hidden trail
with two young men behind,
having convinced them both to follow
with a promise of something real.

One of them hated the man
for bringing him closer to an offer of fate.
He didn't listen when told where to go
and took a wrong step,
losing his mind all at once
without noticing at all.
The subtlest waves of turmoil
crept into his head
as he continued ambling behind.

The other shot darts
into the back of the man's head,
spitting with his tongue
only doubts he wished away.
He didn't believe,
or maybe didn't want to,
that the answers he'd been promised
could be found somewhere like this.
His curiosity drove him still
to continue through the ruins.

The two of them were strangers,
and the man was their stalker,
sliding in between the walls
to get a glimpse of what he wanted.

It was from yearning,
which held a hand across his mouth
as he fought against it
every single day.
He struggled to remember
that his arm was the one
keeping it glued there in place.

As they neared upon the entrance,
the man reflected on his life
how it had changed
since he first came here.
Bygone were the days
where hiding outside could help him get by.
All he saw when he was home
was an endless gray tomorrow,
the wife, the drooping house,
the drooling child moving pictures
with her eyes from across the living room—
he feared the worst for himself
whenever he was there,
and so he left them on occasion
to visit his own sanctuary,
this one on the inside,
taking men like himself
to prove he wasn't alone.

But he never seemed to realize
that he'd been stuck on the inside
since the moment he entered
that crumbled doorway,
swallowing nails and hearing voices,
talking to himself
as if this was the way he had always been.
He didn't know how easy it would be
to simply step outside,
and he honestly didn't mind.
He never really wanted to remember
what it was like anyway.

So forward, and forward,
through the darkness until he felt it,
the hidden life inside the broken building,
as it spoke to him, he's sure,
hearing its words through the phone
that rang from an empty room inside.

It was then that his breath
began to turn to water,
and he another man,
like any of the others he had taken there before.
Watching the windows shatter out
and piece themselves back together,
he cried out for a purpose,
for an answer from inside.

But it didn't speak,
and it didn't move,
for it never really had to;
the thing had been with him all this time,
meeting him wherever he crept
to find his sense of meaning.

Still, he craved it,
he couldn't release it,
even as it dug through his insides,
as it spoke deep inside of him,
this thing he hunted down
and thought about nonstop.
He just couldn't live with the fact
that he'd never looked it in the eyes.
Oh, but it won't stop now,
and it won't stay the same—
his body holds still
while the other's shape moves
every single day.

So he stalked it to the death,
to feel that moment once again—
yes, he starved himself thin,
until the very bitter end.
And when the men behind him
had both disappeared
he was stuck in there alone,
never having bothered
to remember the way back out.

Aisle 16

Heather Hein

"ARE YOU READY TO GO YET?" MY WIFE ASKS ME FOR THE THOUSANDTH TIME IT seems. She's so impatient, but I guess that's just the Aries in her. We were made from different bolts of cloth, my wife and I. I think that's what makes our relationship work for as long as it has. We've put up with each other for twenty-six years now, and I don't suppose my imagined flaws are likely to improve in the near future. She's not flawless either. There are tons of things that she does that bug me. But right now, I have to give her some kind of answer or she's going to get more and more frustrated with me. And we're trying to get out of town for our anniversary—late this year but not the first time. So, I try to placate my wife by telling her I will just be in Home Depot for a few minutes. She doesn't think that we need to stop and get the L brackets for the shelves she doesn't know I finally built for her before we leave, but I want everything to be together so I can put them up as soon as we get home.

She asked me if I was ready to go while I was sitting on the toilet. She asked me if I was ready to go when I was in the shower. She asked me if I was ready to go while I was packing the car. She asked me if I was ready to go while I was making a sandwich. That one really got her. I tried to explain that I was hungry, but it didn't seem to matter to her. She asked me if I was ready to go while I watered the plants, insisting that they weren't going to die during the three days we would be gone. She was actually sitting in the driver's seat of the car seething by the time I got in the car. She didn't say anything on the way to Home Depot.

Now she sits in the driver's seat with her lips pursed, smoking anger radiating off of her shoulders. I tell her I will be right back. She doesn't say anything. Her hands grasp the steering wheel, knuckles white, and I can see that her nails are digging into the palms of her hands. I know that as soon as we get on the road, her anger will dissipate, and we will have a great weekend mountain getaway. She's been waiting for this trip, and we had to put it off twice—first because one of the kids got strep throat and no one wanted to take our disease-riddled children. Second because I had an emergency at work. She looks over at me and says, "Someday I'm going to die waiting for you. You'll come back and I'll be nothing but a corpse!" But she says it in a humorous way that lets me know she's still on the good side of fury. This is one of her favorite lines when she's tired of waiting. If I can just get in and out really quick, she won't stay mad. I pat her hand, tell her I will get her a Coke while I'm there, and her face slackens almost imperceptibly.

I walk quickly into the front door of Home Depot so that she won't be mad about how slow I'm moving. Once those doors whoosh closed behind me, I return to a realistic pace and walk toward the brackets. She's waited for these shelves and I can't wait to give them to her. These aren't plain old shelves. These were built by me out of beautiful walnut and carved by a local artisan with calla lilies—her favorite flower. The finish is velvety soft and will be perfect to display her mother's antique glass figurines. They've been sitting in the shipping box for three years since her parents died, just waiting for a safe place to display them. She's going to love them—I can't wait to see her face when she opens the package they're wrapped in!

I'm in Home Depot at least three times a week as a builder, and my wife claims to detest it. She says she can never find what she wants even when she knows what she needs. So, this is my domain. I usually bring our dog Ponch in here with me and he knows all of the staff. They even have biscuits at the checkout desk. Clark says hello as I walk past, and then Jeremy walks over and shakes my hand. Jeremy had a big problem with the roof replacement he had done by a hack roofing company, and I had hooked him up with a good lawyer he could use to sue the company and get his roof replaced—again—by a reputable company. "That guy you sent me to was great," he says. "We actually won our case last week and I contacted that roofing company you suggested. They came out to do an estimate and I was pretty happy with what I got. It's higher than the other job, but they also have to pay for the drywall damage."

"I'm glad it worked out for you!" I say. "They've screwed over so many people in this community; I can't wait for them to go out of business." I know that's a bad thing to say about another building trade company, but in this case it's true. I don't do roofs, but I used to and I see so many problems it makes me crazy. Sometimes I think it would be financially lucrative to go back into roofing, but I'm not willing to cut the corners it would take to even compete in the bidding process. "They aren't the only company that hires illegals and underpays them. In fact, they replaced the roof on the house I live in now right before we moved in. It was leaking after the first snow and when I got up there to look at it, I saw so many mistakes. Nail holes in the shingles, flashing on upside down, and they didn't strip off the original roof! Just shingled right over the top of it."

"No shit?" Jeremy asks. "What'd you do?"

"Wasn't much I could do about it. The roof was put on for the previous owner and it basically canceled the warranty."

"You're kidding me! Is that even legal?"

"Yep," I say. "It happens all the time. That's why my warranties on skylights stay with the house as long as they haven't been screwed with by anybody. It's a shitty way to do business, but if your goal is to make as much money as you can as fast as you can and then cut and run, it's a good business to be in."

Jeremy looks at me a bit worshipfully, which makes me a little uncomfortable, but also stokes my ego just a little, which I can't say I hate. "Well, when this is all over and I have some money left over, I'll be calling you for some skylights." He claps me on the shoulder the way that guys do, and I give him my business card.

"Just let me know when you're ready and I'll try to cut a deal for you," I say. Jeremy takes the card and gives me a little mock salute before he shambles down the fixtures aisle, his girth making him look more like a Winnebago than a man. But he's a good guy, and he's been working here for a long time. I turn my attention back to the task at hand. What am I here for? Oh, I need a new faucet for the kitchen sink. Ours has a terrible habit of switching to the open spray setting, which does nothing but spray the user in the face. I've been meaning to replace it for months, and I may as well grab it while I'm thinking about it. Besides, Daria will be thrilled if I get started on it when we get back on Sunday afternoon. I should just have enough time to work on it.

I walk down the plumbing aisle and find the selection of faucets for kitchens. The one we have is fake gold and Daria hates it. She says that gold tone is way too '80s and that we should be switching to more flat, muted finishes. This means that I am going to be asked to change all the door knobs, cupboard door pulls, switch plates, outlet covers, and fixtures. Which is expensive, even though she doesn't realize it. So, I find a few that she might like, and after reading the product information on three different boxes, I pick the one with the most water efficiency. That will please her. She's an environmentalist to the core. But now I wonder if the eventual switching out of handles and door knobs will match the finish on the faucet. She's going to ask me about it, so I better check. I head over to the hardware section and gaze at the displays of handles and knobs. I see a couple that she had said she liked, and I check the finish for a good match. It's terrible. Too shiny. So, I trek back to the plumbing section and grab the other one. It's not as efficient, but she won't be reminded of that every time she opens the cupboard over the sink. What she will notice is the fact that the finishes don't match. Just to be sure, I go back to the knob display and actually pull the faucet out of the box. It's a pretty good match.

As I'm about to walk away, my eye catches the price tag on the knobs. They are $3.47 each. To my wife, that wouldn't seem like much. But there are twenty-eight knobs on the cupboards, not to mention door knobs, and all the other stuff that adds up. I can't get all of these at once today. In fact, I will probably only be able to afford a few at a time. Which will probably drive my wife nuts because then they won't match at all. And there's nothing actually wrong with the ones that we have, other than she doesn't like them. But sometimes I realize my wife knows more than I do about things that matter and I should listen to her. So, I grab the twenty-eight cabinet knobs and call it an anniversary gift.

I'm about to walk down the aisle and I see the neighbor who lives behind us. He's renting a firewood splitter, which is something we had talked about splitting the cost of and sharing for a weekend. Apparently, Alex has decided that he doesn't want to wait around and is going ahead without me. And there's no way I can split firewood this weekend when we are supposed to be up in the mountains relaxing all weekend. So, this is irritating to me, but instead I say, "Hey! Getting a start on the splitting?"

"Yeah," Alex says. "Got to make hay while the sun shines and it's supposed to be a great weekend. Daria said you guys were going to be gone for the weekend and I know that it's going to snow next week, so I really wanted to get going."

"Bummer," I say. "I was hoping to get some of that done myself." Then, calculating how long it will take us to get home from Steamboat, I say, "I think we can be home by two on Sunday if we hustle." Cutting our weekend short will most definitely not make my wife happy, but having split firewood will. And it's just a few hours, so it shouldn't be a big deal. I hope. "So, I can chip in for a third of the cost and use it Sunday, then I will bring it back on Monday morning." Alex brightens at this. He's not a bad guy. Interesting cat, in fact—especially if you factor in the pot forest in his backyard that grows every summer. But it's not hurting anything, and I guess it's a good example to my kids that not every person who uses drugs is some scary back alley hoodlum.

"We got a whole tree that we took down this spring, and then there's that tree from Mrs. Marten's yard—fell on the fence last spring. Crushed the shit out of it. Lots of wood to split. But it'll be nice to have this winter. *Farmer's Almanac* says it's gonna be heavy with snow this year." If it's in the *Almanac* (Alex's one and only religious tome), you can believe that Alex will plan accordingly. Alex is like a guy born in the wrong era, or in his case, eras. We're the same age, but he dresses like he's on his way to Woodstock—an event that happened three years before either of us roamed the earth. He hoards scraps and other potentially useful items on the northwest corner of his property like a Depression-era farmer, but I can't see it from my house, so I guess I don't really care. All of his vehicles are gas guzzlers from the 1980s and he frequently pines for the days of Reagan and Bush the First. You can hear the gentle strains of Willie Nelson and Johnny Cash one day, and then hear Led Zeppelin and Black Sabbath for weeks after that. Once I even heard him playing Daft Punk while he was deconstructing something very loud and very large in his garage one weekend.

I have to carry this conversation out to its inevitable end, because Alex won't let me escape until he's done. So, I listen quietly while he rails against the Obama administration, praises Trump, predicts that socialism is on the rise, espouses the virtues of Ayn Rand, and asks me when I'm going to start purchasing American-made cars. I won't bother telling him that most foreign cars are actually manufactured right here in the United States. This will just prolong the discussion and I really need to get going so Daria and I can get on the road. Alex ends his oration by telling me to watch out for hitchhiking illegals on the way to Steamboat. I don't bother to tell him that illegals can't afford Steamboat getaways, whether they hitch or not, and the white-bread mountain folk aren't likely to hire them for ski slope jobs. As a way of saying goodbye he high-fives me and tells me to keep up the good fight.

As I stand there watching his retreating figure, I realize that my hands are sweating and all the plastic bags holding the door knobs are damp with sweat. I walk to the front of the store and grab a cart so I don't have to keep walking around with them in my hand. Lucy waves to me from register 10, right by the cart corral. She's sweet on me, but she's also sixty, so I cut her some slack. "How's that dog of yours?" she asks and flashes me a smile. The overhead fluorescents reflect off the silver fillings in her molars.

"Ponch? He's in the car with Daria, waiting . . ." Yes. Waiting for me to get what I need and get back into the car. She's no doubt foaming at the mouth by now. "Waiting to take a trip up to the mountains for the weekend. It's our anniversary, and we rented a cabin for the two of us. Three if you count Ponch." She waves the information away like crumbs across the counter. She's always been more fond of my dog than my wife. It might be because every time Daria comes in here her expression is a mixture of "I smell dog shit" and "I have to pee." But I have to shut Lucy down and get on with my mission. I've wasted too much time already. "Sorry, Luce, I got to get what I need and get out to the car." She makes a face like I farted on her counter, and I smile my most winning smile at her as I walk away. I got off easy.

Okay, heading straight to the brackets now. They're in aisle 16. I make a right and walk to the middle of the aisle, but it looks like they have moved the brackets and other hanging fixtures to another location. But here are the towel rods that Daria liked. They, of course, match the same brushed nickel finish as the knobs in the cart. The cart! I left it with Lucy. I walk quickly back to the front of the store to get the cart and wink at Lucy. "Forgot the cart," I say as a way of second greeting.

"I guess you did." She smiles and crosses her arms over her ample bosom. She gives me a look of disapproval and what could become love if given time and circumstance. I'm aware of her eyes fixing on my butt as I walk away from her. I walk back down toward aisle 16, but I walk right past it and turn down 17 instead. The brackets weren't in that aisle anyway. Here again are the towel rods I had been looking at. I must have chosen the wrong aisle the first time and the brackets really are in aisle 16 like I thought. I look at the two different variations of towel rods and pick the heavier one that seems to be sturdier. I throw it in the cart and then push it down the aisle to make my way toward 16. Then I realize that she's going to want two so we can replace both of them in the bathroom instead of having a new one and old one clashing with each other. I back up and go back toward the towel rods. They only have one in the style I had chosen. So, I can wait until later, choose the lighter version, or go ask to see if they have more in the back. I know that Daria will be happy to have the towel rods, so I find the nearest orange apron.

The nearest orange apron happens to be Tad, short for Tadlock Downing III, son of Tadlock Downing II, son of Terrence Jefferson Downing. There was no Tad the First, he has told me. He's a good kid, working through college. His knowledge and work ethic have impressed me so much that I've made a decision to offer him a job with my company. Joyce, my office manager, and I had discussed it a few weeks ago, and we both agreed that this would be a good time to start him out and see how he does. This is the first time I've seen him since that conversation, and if I don't bring it up now, I'll forget. "Hey, Tad!" I say, sunny smile blazing on my face. "I wonder if you can check to see if you have another towel rod like this in the back." I show him the box and he looks at it with concentration.

"To tell you the truth, I don't think I've ever even seen this item in the store. Where did you find it?"

"It was in aisle seventeen with the other hanging rods," I say. Tad's brows knit together and he's reading the box, tracing his finger along as he reads. He looks like a pharmacist double-checking his work before giving over the drugs to a patient.

"I don't know . . . like I said, I never seen this one before. Let me go take a look." I follow him back to aisle 17, but that's where the cupboard door knobs are hanging. Am I this screwed up? He looks at me questioningly. “You sure you found it here? I don’t see any.” I’m not sure anymore.

“Maybe they were in the next aisle over. I was looking at the cupboard door knobs earlier.” I motion to the basket of the cart, but there are no brushed nickel cupboard door knobs in the cart. Tad raises an eyebrow at me and motions for me to follow him. We pass aisle 18, 17, 16, and then he turns down aisle 15. As I round the corner I stop short, and suddenly, there’s no Tad Orange Apron in sight. But he was just here in front of me. I shake my head—he must have turned down 16 and I wasn’t paying attention. I turn the cart around and turn down aisle 16. No Tad. But here are the towel rods! I no longer have the original one I picked up because Tad is currently wandering around the store with it. I look at the boxes and see at least a dozen of the type I was looking for in the first place. I grab another one and go to seek out Tad so I can show it to him and get the other one back. When I get back to the main thoroughfare, there’s no Tad.

I stand where I am for a minute, close my eyes, and massage my temples. I’m beginning to get a headache. When I open my eyes again, Tad is standing there holding the box with the towel rod in it. It’s like he materialized in front of me instead of walking up to me. I give a muffled not-quite-a-scream of surprise and then I laugh. Tad doesn’t laugh. He asks me if I’m okay. “Yes, I’m fine,” I say. “Did you find it?” I ask. “Because I found another one—there was a whole stack of them just down aisle 16.” I motion to the basket of my cart to the other one, but the other one isn’t in the cart, even though I just put it in there, not even a minute ago! “Wait,” I say. “It was right here!” Tad looks at me with his trademark seriousness, but now the look has a touch of worry and, lurking in the back, fear. *Yeah, Tad,* I think. *Better look out because Mr. Havens is losing his mind.* “Did you find one?” I ask to take the focus off my questionable mental state and back to the matter at hand.

“Well, it’s like I said, Mr. Havens. We don’t actually carry this product. I don’t even know how this got here because there’s no record of this CPU code anywhere in the system, archived or otherwise. I even checked the national database and I don't see that it's in any of our stores."

"That doesn't make any sense, though. I found like twelve of them right down there!" I wave toward aisle 16, the one I have just emerged from. But as I follow the hand movement with my gaze, I see that I'm standing in front of aisle 6. Aisle 6 is full of trim boards. I know I never went down there. I look back at Tad, who has taken an appreciable step away from the unraveling Mr. Havens standing in front of him. "Well that's weird," I say, trying for aloof self-deprecation. I smile my winning sales smile and Tad echoes it back, but it's not convincing. "Come on, I'll show you."

Tad follows me at a distance back down to aisle 16, which turns out to be lighting fixtures. I stop short and look at him, trying to keep the sudden panic out of my face. It is a mask of complete calm, but that's not what it feels like underneath. It feels like eels are swimming in my intestines. I'm sweating now, and I realize that I forgot to put on my deodorant before we left, even though Daria reminded me. I can smell myself, and I smell like pizza. Gross. Tad points down aisle 16. "That's not where we keep the rods and stuff, Mr. H. You'll find those down aisle seventeen." Too much time has passed now. I can't spend any more time looking.

"Never mind, Tad. I'm in a little bit of a hurry, so I'll just skip it until next time." Tad shakes his head at me and watches me carefully. "Can you remind me where I can find shelf brackets?"

Tad looks a little more than relieved to have this lunatic out of his face, so he points down the causeway and says, "Aisle twenty-two. Shelving and hardware."

"Thanks, Tad!" I say, more chipper than the situation warrants. He is still looking at me with concern. I give him the friendly wave and push the cart toward aisle 22. I look in the cart and see that there is a strange array of items I do not remember putting in there. The faucet is still there. That's good. Reality check number one. The cupboard door handles are in there too. Good. Reality check number two. There are two brushed nickel heavy-duty towel rods in there too, but that does nothing to help cement reality for me. I never had two of them in the cart at all. When I look more closely though, I see that the faucet I have is bright silver, not the brushed nickel I had chosen. I groan inwardly, knowing that Daria is probably screaming silently in the car right now.

I push the cart back down the main causeway again and don't bother with aisle numbers, I just go until I find the faucets. I reach into the cart to exchange the one I accidentally grabbed, but then I see it *is* the right one. "Brushed nickel, Flow Motion Activated Single Handle Pull Down Sprayer Kitchen Faucet with Motion Sensor." Yep, that's the right one. But a minute ago it wasn't the right one. I could swear it. I'm just standing here now in aisle . . . aisle what? I look up and see I'm now in aisle 49. As far as I know, there is no aisle 49 in Home Depot. But maybe I'm wrong. I put the faucet back in the cart and walk back to the main thoroughfare that I had just come from.

What I see is not possible. There is no end to this corridor in front of me. I can't believe it at first, so I look away back to where I just came from. Shelving. Brackets. Brackets! I push the cart, almost running behind it now, and find the right brackets for the job. Great. Brackets found, now let's go, I tell myself. I spin the cart around to head back out to the front of the store, but there's a display where the front of the store should be. It's a display I've never seen in here before, but it's beautifully done. Against my better judgment (time's ticking, after all), I am drawn forward, cart forgotten.

What I see is grass, and stone, and a waterfall. It's beautiful! Somehow they got grass to grow into the concrete. There's a path leading to what looks like a courtyard. It's a circular display with an X cut through, dividing the sections of impossible grass into four pie-shaped wedges. Each one is as big as my front yard. Stone planter beds have been constructed, and inside each of them are the most beautiful calla lilies I've ever seen. Not just white, but deep purple, yellow, indigo, red, and some colors I don't even have words for, because I have never seen them before. I go to take my phone out to get a picture for Daria, but I left it back in the car.

Something out of the corner of my right eye catches my attention. On the other side of the cobbled path is another stone planter, but this one is filled with carnivorous plants. Jude, the youngest of my brood, is obsessed with carnivorous plants. He got one for his birthday last year but forgot to take care of it and it died. There are little Venus flytraps like the one he had, but there are also pitcher plants. Huge pitcher plants, big enough to catch a small mammal or bird. I lean over to smell them—they are beautiful and red and glistening. But they don't smell good. In fact, they smell like garbage. Another plant next to the pitchers looks like nothing I've ever seen before. The little tag in the dirt identifies it as a Drosera Sundew. These are as big as my fist and are also glistening with what looks like dew. There are at least a dozen of these, and when I look closer, I see that various insects are in the process of decomposition and look like acid is eating them from the bottom up. A grasshopper looks at me with its alien eye, silently imploring me to help. I examine it more closely and see that half of it has already been eaten away and I cannot help.

I turn my head away from this carnage, feeling sick and dizzy from whatever garbage-y perfume is wafting through the air and invading my nostrils. I back away from the planter and almost trip over a board and iron bench that's been placed there. Next to it is a lamp post. Underneath the lamp post a colony of mushrooms has been placed there, but they aren't the fake lawn décor mushrooms. These are real, but unreal. They are spotted like cartoons. They are arranged in a spiral from smallest to largest, and I can just barely see tiny footprints on them. Not animal footprints, but little girl's shoes, as if a little girl about ten inches high had been using them as a stairway. I sit down on the bench—hard enough that my teeth click together. This isn't even like an acid trip. It's like a bad dream that I can't wake up from.

Wait—maybe I am dreaming. Maybe all of this is just a dream. But the smells coming from those plants and the colors I see can't be a product of my own imagination, can they? I close my eyes for a few moments and try to slow my breathing. Across the way, in the opposite pie wedge I can see movement in the grass. At this point my fear is beginning to swell, but I move forward toward the grass anyway. It's like I'm being piloted by some other intelligence that feels hard and impersonal. "Come see my wares," the intelligence seems to say. The ground is rolling. It's like a Bugs Bunny cartoon animal is burrowing and the grass swells like Astroturf. On the opposite side, a prehistoric green horror picture show raises its head and makes eye contact with me. There was some song in the seventies about alligator lizards in the air. As a kid I didn't know what an alligator lizard was, but now that I see it in front of me, the disturbing image that song had always conjured in my mind has appeared.

This dark green creature is at least ten feet long. Its head looks like that of a snake, and indeed its body resembles a snake's, but it also has legs. Not four legs, but hundreds, like a centipede. It's round, as big as a dinner plate, and the thing's mouth is at least a foot long, ending like an alligator's snout. As it yawns, I can see rows of pointed teeth. Its tail whips back and forth, and I can't help myself. I just stand there, transfixed in numb, disgusted horror as it looks at me. A curious sort of intelligence radiates from its eyes, black and dead and sinister.

Finally, the spell breaks and just as the creature begins to run across the mysterious grass lawn, I'm able to stumble away and I begin to run down the path. I run for what seems like ten minutes before I get to the end of the path and I see aisle 16 again. When I dare to look behind me to see if the thing has caught up, it's not there. Nothing is there. No display, no flowers, no carnivorous plants, no alligator lizard. It's the wall of the store. I can see the double doors that open on the area where they sell large patio furniture and paving stones. I don't see any employees when I look through the doors, and they don't open automatically like they should. I need to find an orange apron. I need to find out what is going on.

I look back over my shoulder and see the aisles lined up just as they should be. I can hear the conversations at the front of the store as people pay for their purchases and exchange small talk with the cashiers. I'm pretty sure I can even hear Lucy's gravelly smoker's laugh. I look up at the aisle numbers and see that they are all labeled as aisle 16. When I look back toward the double doors, the display is back again. It's dark there now, the lights above are off, and the display has been lit by walkway lights. A large pergola has been constructed and rope lights are hanging there, casting a soft light that doesn't go beyond the center of the display, making it impossible to see into the patches of green grass where anything could be lurking. I can hear that thing hissing, so I take off running toward the aisles.

I'm completely panicked now. All I want is to get out of this place, find Daria, and get going. Whatever this is—hallucination, dream, reality—I don't care. I take off running and look down each aisle as I pass it. They're all labeled 16. I turn down the first one, heading to what is surely the front of the store. I stop suddenly. This is not the shelving aisle, the bathroom fixtures, or anything that could possibly be sold at the Home Depot. On both sides of the aisle, enclosed in glass cases, are medical instruments. They range from tiny scalpels to larger saws to decapitation shears. I can see that they aren't all new, and they aren't all clean. Some have a black substance on them. Some look like they have clumps of hair stuck to them. They are displayed on white covered boards and there's . . . what, sinew? Long trails of bloody material are splayed across some of the boards. I walk farther down the aisle, and I can see that now there are organs, pieces of flesh, some covered in hair like an animal's, some in scales. I don't want to see this anymore!

I keep running toward the front of the store, blind panic now engulfing all of my senses. All I want is to get out. What I don't want is to see any more. I hang a left at the next aisle and am not surprised to see that it's aisle 16. This version is selling vintage clothing. Top hats and velvet jackets fly by as I run. I come to another junction and turn right. I'm confronted with what looks like zoo enclosures. Animals I've never seen lurk in their confinements. Some of them look like comical splices of different animals stuck together by an evil child. Dogs with leathery wings of bats, only much bigger, the back half of their bodies missing, trail blood and other worse looking substances. Entrails? I don't want to know. I keep on running.

I figure if I make a left and then a right, followed by left and right over and over again, I should make it to where the front entrance is. The next aisle (16 of course) houses chains, power tools, and huge metal hooks from which dangle bloodied pieces of animals I can't begin to identify. I fly past these without looking too carefully—I don't want to see any more. I run with my eyes closed and smack right into an orange apron—Tad! "Agh! Jesus Christ, help me!" I plead with Tad. But he doesn't react. He doesn't look at me. His eyes are gone and in their place is nothing but obsidian darkness. The alien eye of the grasshopper in the plant. I shake him, but when his mouth begins to open, I realize I don't want to see or hear anything that may come out of it. I shove Tad to the side and keep running. The only lights in the store now are the garden path lights, which lend the place the air of some other world. I can hear the sounds of foreign animals behind me and I see things moving in the darkness beyond the lights. Shapeless movements of unknown creatures.

Finally, I see daylight! I smash through the automatic doors, thinking they would have opened for me, but they didn't. I'm covered with cuts and scrapes, bleeding, and heaving breaths. I lean over and vomit. The daylight is so bright it hurts my eyes. I have a stab of pain through the right side of my head like a lightning bolt. The car! I see the car! It's the only one in the parking lot. I rush to it and see Daria in the driver's seat and Ponch in the back, sleeping. Her head is back against the head rest like she is asleep. The doors are locked and the windows are fogged over. I get my keys out of my pocket, screaming her name at the top of my lungs. Why doesn't she hear me? Can't she see? I wrench the door open and am struck by the same smell of the carnivorous plants in the store display. Daria isn't sleeping and neither is the dog. They are just rotting shapes of corpses. Jesus, something got to them too! I reach in and touch her face, which crumbles to powder. They are . . . ancient, it seems. But how could that be??

I reach into the center console and pull out my cell phone. When I open it, I notice the date: it's still October 10, but the year is fifty years from when I left the car and went into the store. I open it to call 911, but nothing works. I look at myself in the mirror and am shocked to see that my face is deeply trenched with wrinkles. My dark hair, once thick, is now just wispy milkweed fluff. I slide into the passenger seat, put my hands over my face, and begin to cry.

I Can't Believe I Didn't See This Coming

Mary E. Monte

We used to capture souls for fun
Cackling in the night at those we held hostage
Awake for days on chemical euphoria
Tripping over tombstones in the local cemetery

I can't believe I watched
You tie your knots and call it friendship
You tighten your grip in the name of sisterhood
Douse me with cheap vodka under the guise of love

My bare feet shift against splintered wood
Nine years past and you've got me strapped—
The hard reality of your stake pressed against my spine,
I can't believe I didn't see this coming.

So here we are
Engulfed by your path of destruction
Asphyxiated by your empty promises
Doomed to burn for all of eternity in the hell of your creation

In the aftermath of you and me
I sort through our remains
You tried to burn me alive,
But I am a child of the flames.

The Other Day

D.S. Waldman

The other day I pilfered lavender
From my neighbor's garden without asking,
A fistful, so sweet in its springtime bloom,
Bagged it and mailed it across the country
To Brooklyn, NYC, to a woman,
The only woman for whom I would pick
Lush, glowing, pollen-frosted lavender
Without holding onto some for myself
(okay, I did keep one of the mauve buds,
Which I slipped into a champagne glass
Where it can drink atop my writing desk).
She's also the only woman for whom
I would knowingly and willingly
Skirt the fringes of romantic cliché.

Also the other day, after heavy rain,
A towering oak tree lifted from its roots
And crashed down in a rogue wave of timber,
Leveling the greenhouse, the carport,
The storage shed, the neighbor's camper
(which sat, sparsely used, beneath the carport
For as long as I've known them to have it),
And settled with its sprawling hulk of limbs

In a calamitous snarl across the yard,
Falling only several feet short of
The lavender bush where earlier I knelt
With clippers, harvesting romantic hope
To send to Ms. X over in Brooklyn.
They've begun sawing the arms from the tree
And sky has filled the space it used to occupy.

You can see the bottom of the oak now,
Upturned, its roots splaying out through black soil;
You'd have expected something more substantial,
Roots like garden hoses snaking about,
But this sky-tickling centenarian
Was anchored with little more than twine
Woven down a few feet into the earth.
—I suppose this is where I could dovetail
The improbability of love
With the triumph of giant oak trees
Growing despite such fragile foundations,
Where I could paint my picking and sending
Of lavender to Ms. X in Brooklyn
As the delicate roots of our romance
That will one day anchor our oak of love.

Yes, the thirsty timber of longing,
The rich, endless humus of passion,
The wandering limbs of love's trajectory;
I'm certain this poem has been written,
But I've exhausted my store of tree-words
And am also hesitant to tie a neat bow
At poem's end when, after all, the damn tree fell!
(the devastation of aborted romance—?)

Ms. X might very well be spoken for;
It's been several years since we last shared space
And I hear that living in New York City
Is basically a process of falling
Incessantly in and out of love,
So the odds are stacked against me—stacked like
The clean-sawed blocks of white oak outside my house.

And perhaps it's all okay—trees falling,
Things breaking, chainsaws wailing for days;
Love going unrequited, lavender
Arriving in the mail stiff and scentless.
I kneel and run my finger along the
Craggy contours of the dark-granite bark,
Thacher Creek flowing happily below,
Sounding like a chubby serpent sliding
Forever over a bed of dry leaves.
A private avenue of gilded sunlight
Finds me through the leaves of unfallen trees,
Warming my hair from lifetimes away.
Above, two hummingbirds mating,
Goosed together in a raucous flutter,
Unbridled in this most natural impulse.

The Day I Met My Mother

Patsy Lally

MY MOTHER IS BETTY CROCKER, THE WOMAN WHO MAKES THE CAKE MIXES YOU see in the grocery store. I haven't seen her since the day social services barged into our apartment and dragged me away. A large policeman held me tight. I cried and fought and called for her, but the other police took Mama and Uncle Daddy away. After that I don't remember much. Lots of foster homes, lots of different families, some nice, some not so much.

The day I found out what had happened to my mother, my new foster mother was making a chocolate cake for her daughter's birthday. This foster mother liked to cook. Usually her kitchen smelled of garlic, onions, and beans simmering in a large pot on the stove. Today it only smelled sweet.

On the table was a tiny, brown bottle. "What's that?" I asked.

"Vanilla," she said.

"Can I sniff it?" I picked up the bottle before she answered and sniffed. It smelled like it should be the most delicious thing in the world. I knew better.

"But you should never drink it," I said.

"Did you ever drink it?" she asked.

"Yuk, it tasted terrible. My mother was making a cake for my birthday, and after I spit her vanilla out she went to get Uncle Daddy's bottle of gin for the cake. Mama took a big gulp before she poured a bunch into the chocolate frosting."

"Who was Uncle Daddy?"

That's when I stopped talking. Foster mothers told social workers everything you said. Then it went into a big notebook. You had to be careful.

"Just one of Daddy's brothers who came around after Daddy left." I shrugged to show it wasn't important. She waited, but I stayed quiet.

Then she said, "What happened to the cake?"

"Well, when Mama poured the chocolate icing over the cake, it just kept moving, over the cake and onto the table. Some even dripped on the floor. Mama laughed and laughed and so I laughed too. Mama hugged me and twirled me around." I didn't tell her the rest. I didn't tell her that my mama promised, "Sugar, next time I'm gonna make you the best chocolate cake in the world."

"You puttin' candles on the cake so your little girl can make a wish?" I asked.

"Of course," she said, "and next month when you're eight I'll put candles on yours so you can make a wish too."

Maybe a wish on birthday candles might be better. Every night I made a wish on the first star in the night sky. It was always the same wish. I wanted my mama to come and get me so we could laugh again. Even without the messy cake, so far that had been my best birthday ever.

On the kitchen counter a colorful red and yellow box caught my eye. It was the cake mix box, and on it was the picture of a smiling, happy woman in a red dress with a clean, white collar and a string of pearls. The woman in the picture had brown hair and red lips. I recognized her right away. "That's my mother," I said.

"No, that's Betty Crocker," said my foster mother.

But it was my mother, I knew it. Now I understood. I had to be in foster care because of how busy she was with the cake mixes and all. She did love me, but I was just one little girl, and there were so many children who needed the comfort of sweetness in their lives. But my foster mother just gave me her sad, tired smile and a piece of toast.

"You are such a silly child," she said. "You're too old to be daydreaming all the time."

I told some kids at school about my mother, but they just laughed. I knew it was hard for them to believe, but I believed it and for a long time, and through many foster homes, it was the soft blanket of angel food that covered me every night as I dreamed of my mother.

TODAY IS MY EIGHTEENTH birthday. That's the day you have to leave the foster care system. My brown cardboard suitcase had already been packed the night before. This foster mother was in a hurry for me to move along. She was expecting another child this afternoon. I'd been in this home for three years. Mrs. Burke hadn't been mean, she hadn't been kind, she just didn't even seem to know I was there. A few years ago someone gave me a small teddy bear as a Christmas gift. I took it out of my suitcase and sat it on the bed. Maybe it would help the new kid not feel so alone. The first night in a new home is always the hardest.

A taxi took me from Mrs. Burke's house to my meeting with Mrs. Neudecker, the social worker who had been seeing me for the past few years. I sat at her desk, not able to stop my knees from bouncing up and down while she asked me lots of questions about what I was going to do now. I didn't hear her questions, but politely waited until she was finished. Then I told her I wanted to see my mother. I told her I wouldn't be any trouble, and I could even help my mother with her work. She stared at me for a moment, head tilted to one side like a puppy when it's trying to make sense of what you're saying. She looked through my rather thick file. Finally, she took out a document, looked at it, and looked at me for what seemed like a long time.

"That might not be such a good idea," she said. She smiled when she said it, but her eyes looked like the old basset hound in one of my foster homes. She looked sad. I didn't know why.

"It's all I've ever wanted; I can't do anything else until I've met my mother."

"Why not get settled in a place to live, maybe find a job first. I've got a list of jobs for a good girl like you."

"No. I want to meet my mother."

"You look very pretty today," she said as she looked at my red jumper, white blouse with collar, and a string of pearls I had bought in Walmart. I was dressed like the picture of my mother on the cake mix boxes. It would be our mother and daughter outfit.

She wrote down a name and address on an index card. While she was writing, she kept glancing up at me. I could tell she didn't really want to give me the address, but I didn't care. It was the one thing I had promised myself I would do as soon as I could.

I took the card and looked at the name. It said "Betty Cornfield."

"You've spelled her name wrong," I said, placing the card back on the desk.

She looked at the card and then at me.

"No, I didn't," she said. "That's her name and this is the last address we have for her."

Written at the top of the card was Nell's Kitchen. I saw by the address I didn't know that part of town. I thought maybe it was where the factories were, you know where they add ingredients to the flour and turn out the different kinds of cake mixes.

"Thank you," I said as I took the card.

Mrs. Neudecker stood and came around her desk. She hugged me, pulling me into her ample bosom. It felt like being enveloped into a Sunday morning warm cinnamon roll. She gave me some money, some from a metal box in her drawer and some from her own purse, and wished me good luck.

"Don't be scared," she said. I guess she'd read in my file that I was scared a lot. I was never as clever as my foster parents' real children or even some of the other foster kids who paraded in and out of my life over the years. Everyone called me a daydreamer.

They weren't wrong; I dreamed about my mother every day.

She looked into my eyes. Her deep, brown eyes were like chocolate kisses. Keeping her hands on my shoulders, she said I could make a life for myself and good things could come my way. She told me to remember that freedom meant choices. She said that I'd been a good girl and now there were things I needed to do, places I needed to go. She asked me to come back to see her after I'd met my mother. I promised that I would, but I kept two fingers crossed. That made the promise not binding. I was finally going to meet my mother. My heart was full and bubbly like the froth on an ice cream soda. As nice as she was, I hoped I'd never need to see Mrs. Neudecker again.

I TOOK A TAXI to the address on the card. I kept smoothing my skirt and patting my hair, opening and closing my purse as if something new might have appeared since the last time. I wanted to look really nice. The taxi came to an area of warehouses with trucks parked alongside and between each. Nell's Kitchen was in a long, narrow building the color of peanut butter. The front had a large window on which menus had been taped. A tall green plant drooped like a sad sentry in one corner of the window. Even the new growth leaves were turning brown. That plant was desperately in need of water. The taxi driver asked me if I was sure this was the place.

"Of course," I said, "it's a test kitchen."

He looked at me real funny, took the money and drove away.

Inside Nell's there were booths on the left side and a counter with stools on the right. The booths and stools were covered with pink leather the color of Pepto Bismol. Someone had taped over cracks and worn spots on the leather seats with black tape. The tape too had cracked bleeding bits of pink plastic. A doorway to the kitchen was behind the counter next to a large window with a shelf for the prepared food. It smelled like burgers and onions. I was surprised, but there were some pies in a glass enclosed cabinet behind the counter, and cakes on the counter covered with clear plastic domes.

There was a fly trapped under an old, scratched cover over a chocolate cake. I watched it circle the cover, looking for a way out. It never landed on the cake. You would think that being trapped with a chocolate cake would be fly paradise. But no, this fly was circling and circling, searching for a way out.

Nell's was full of men eating lunch. I didn't see any women at the counter or in the booths. Most of them turned to look at me as I stood there by the door. They all looked different, yet the same, some bald, some bearded, but almost all had an unbuttoned plaid shirt over a white tee. Most kept chewing, mouths open, food remaining inside except for small particles that escaped unnoticed by the chewer. One or two, with nothing left to chew, just stared. I guess to get the men to test the cakes, they have to offer them some regular lunch first.

A waitress walked from behind the counter and toward me. She was very pale, soft, with a big, round belly. Holding up her large body was a pair of very thin legs. It was like watching a marshmallow on stilts. Over her raspberry-colored uniform, she had tied a small white apron. Grasping at her head was a net that was doing its best to hold down a crown of frizzy red hair.

"Is Betty here?" I said.

"Betty," she shouted over her right shoulder, "somebody to see you."

"Tell him I dropped dead, and he should do the same," said a loud, raspy voice from beyond the counter.

"It's not him," said the redhead, "it's a girl."

For a moment I thought I could turn and run out the door. She didn't know I was coming. She wouldn't even know who the girl was that had asked for her. But my legs wouldn't move, so I just stood still.

A very skinny woman walked out of the kitchen. She may make the cakes, but it was obvious she didn't eat any. Her hair was light brown, like mine. But her hair was so thin and greasy, a hairnet would have had nothing to cling to. Her eyes were brown, like mine, but hers were ringed with black mascara. We had the same face and high cheekbones. But the bottom half of her face was tanned and wrinkled like an apple left out in the sun. Her fingers were orange, I imagined from the many cigarettes she smoked. I could see a pack in her apron pocket. She wore a raspberry-colored uniform identical to the one worn by the redhead. Wiping her hands on a limp, threadbare dishtowel, she stopped and just stared at me.

"Ma," I said. Such a tiny word, just two letters, but I'd waited such a long time to say it. I couldn't help myself so I repeated, "Ma," just like I'd whispered into my pillow so many times. That was the first time I spoke it out loud. I slipped my purse over my shoulder in case she wanted to hug me.

"Well, son of a bitch if it ain't my kid. Sit down, sit down," she said as she took my hand and led me to a booth.

"Dottie, it's my kid," she said to the other waitress.

"I didn't know you had a kid," said Dottie.

"It's a long story," said my mother. "But didn't she turn out pretty."

"Did you bake these cakes?" I asked.

"Nah, we got an old lady in town does that. She's real good though and this bunch loves 'em. Don't you, fellas?" she said to the men who were giving us their full attention. A couple of men nodded and then turned away.

"So, what you doin' here?" she asked.

I guess I thought she would know. She should know it was my birthday. I guess I thought we'd always wanted the same thing.

"It's my birthday, I turned eighteen today."

"You did? Well ain't that nice."

"I wanted to see you. I've wanted to see you for such a long time."

"Oh, sugar," she said. "I'm sure glad to see you. Where you living now?"

"I'm not sure."

"Oh," was all Betty said at first. She looked down at her hands, clasping her orange-stained fingers. Then after a few moments she said, "Well, you see, I live in a small room up the street and most nights a friend might come by, but if you need a place to stay for tonight you can have the couch." Her hand moved unconsciously to the pack of cigarettes in her apron pocket as if just knowing they were there brought comfort.

"I've thought about you all the time," she said. "I was away for a while and when I got back, I asked them social workers about you, but they said I couldn't have you back. They were mean. Was they mean to you, sugar?" she said.

Instead of speaking, I just shook my head.

"Well, I'm glad because I couldn't of stood it if I thought they were mean to my baby girl."

"Is my daddy here?" I asked.

Betty's eyes slid downward. "No, honey, he ain't. I haven't seen him since he got out of jail. But he didn't do nothin' wrong. Them cops framed him."

I watched the fly climbing up and around the inside of the dirty cake cover.

"I don't need a place to stay," I said. "I have places to go."

"Well that's good. Now you listen to your mama, you're real pretty," she said as she leaned across the table and stroked my cheek with one jagged, cracked fingernail. "Don't be giving it away. While you're young and pretty, you make 'em pay for it."

"Well, if you work, you get paid."

"Listen to my little girl, only eighteen and already smarter than her mama ever was. You just make sure."

"Hey, Betty," came a voice from the kitchen, "you got orders to pick up."

"Shut up, shit for brains," she shouted. "This here's my kid and it's her birthday."

A tall man came out of the kitchen. He had black hair and a large mustache. The knot of his hairnet came down to the middle of his forehead. The hairnet thing must be some kind of a rule. But his apron was filthy with brown stains, red stains, and very faded, unidentifiable stains. He looked at me and then back at my mother.

"You got a kid?" he said. "Well, now I've heard it all." He kept shaking his head as he turned and walked back into the kitchen.

"Hey, I'll make you a burger if you like," she said to me.

"No, thank you."

"How about a piece of chocolate cake to celebrate your birthday?"

My throat closed at the thought of taking a bite of anything. But, though I couldn't eat it, I knew once she took the cover off the cake the confused fly could escape, could flee his chocolate paradise. Perhaps he'd thought about it and realized his paradise, if there was such a thing, lay elsewhere. Maybe it was in a place he'd never even thought about as he dreamed only about the abundance in Nell's Kitchen. I just knew that fly had places to go.

"Sure, Betty," I said.

Words as Weapons of War

Arien Reed

I think I'm a transman
The flat horizon of his mouth
Did not shift
And then
Clamped in the irons of denial
He perused the thicket of conversation
Searching for the other path, the better path
I must be on
I must be overreacting, exaggerating
He pushed through all groves of grief
Except anger
As though he was losing someone
Instead of gaining the full me
Then he cut me in turn
No matter the hormones and surgery
You'll never be a true man
I didn't realize coming out
Was a declaration of war
That I had just unbuckled my armor
And pointed to my heart
He looked for proof online
That cishet men can stay without
Being gay

As though life was a prescription
Results of active trials revealed online
"I left her"
Was the general consensus among
Those willing to so much as speak of it
But marriage is forever and love is enduring
Isn't it?

In the end the warrior kicked down all flags
And only breeze stirred the dust at our feet
I love you for who you are
Regardless your gender and body
I stabbed my sword into the earth
And took his empty hand in mine
Knowing I don't deserve this surrender
Any more than the cage I escaped
But we're not telling my parents

The next time I was to visit his family
I donned my binder
Took it off, tried on my old female attire
Hated myself
And took it back off
Naked wasn't an option
And I hate the bright, curved sight of it
So I put my binder back on
And crossed into partially welcome territory

With silence and a smile

A Skin I Shed in Vegas, The Second I Brought Back

Sarah Ann Cohen

Part of me stayed in Vegas;
Skin melted to the asphalt,
Strewn down the strip like curtains—
Soured in the sunlight and brushing the shoulders of passersby
        Gently
Whispering *please will you take me home.*

Nineteen—no fake ID, but fluttering eyelashes;
The glue like cement.
I tore them off on the bathroom floor,
Ripped the real ones
All the wishes I was wasting falling in grout lines—
I'd have put tongue to tile if I could've
Eaten them,
But I left them there instead.
They dug into my knees like splinters.

A girl poured water over my lips,
Left me on that hotel floor,
Said the next night I'm so glad you're okay—
On the way home I thought I was carsick;
Reached down my throat and stood my stomach
On the back of the gas station toilet,
            Swollen and throbbing—
I peeled the insides of it clean
With my fingernails—
I left it there.

The door handle rattled (like unsteady breaths)
While I was taking a shower—
Washing off the bedsheets
Sweat stuck to my stomach
And the side of my face,
Second skin sheets—
            Staining
Like the bruises that softened
Into the skin of my inner thighs
As they would on a rotting fruit—
I was born with bird bones
That splintered when bitten.

The expanse of his back swallowing the spray of water,
Swallowing the ceiling lights,
Shouldering into the room (and eating it, his tongue a siphon,
his teeth cement)
Wider than the walls should've allowed—
He told me
            Gently
You're more fun when you're drunk.

I asked him

please will you take me home—

He said tomorrow.

Part of me stayed in Vegas—
I left it (I let it).
I came home curtained in
new skin.

Good Luck Fox

Casey Gibson

MASARU WAS IN AN ELEVATOR FILLED TO CAPACITY, PRESSED BETWEEN TWO balding business men in identical beige suits. He was pretty sure they were wearing the same pair of clunky, square, black glasses too. The briefcase of the man to Masaru's right was digging into his side, just below his ribs. No matter how many times he moved, the case just ended up digging into the same spot. Which meant that his new suit was going to be wrinkled when he met his new client. Great.

When the doors finally opened to the seventeenth floor of the Royal Hotel Tokyo, Masaru took a few deep breaths and straightened his hair. Well, he tried to anyway, the chestnut curls had a mind of their own and refused to bow to his will. He strode toward Ms. Kayo's room while running over her information in his head once more. She only went by her first name—he hadn't even been given her surname. She was his age—twenty-four. She had checked into her room last night—despite his advice to wait until he had had a chance to inspect it. A celebrity chef. Masaru had been required to memorize how many Instagram subscribers she had—300,000. Her crowning achievement, however, was her YouTube channel, where she had hundreds of videos in Japanese and English, teaching people to cook different recipes—of mostly Japanese food. Her channel had over 9 million subscribers, and between that and her various expositions she had more than enough money to live off of.

Sometimes, YouTube stars could be treated almost like idols. Masaru had certainly seen his fair share of crazy fans whenever he worked with a celebrity. Just last year, he had been hired by another YouTuber visiting from America and had had to escort three people from the premises of the convention, and two from the lobby of his client's hotel.

He shuddered at the thought of the one man who had tattooed his client's face onto his chest.

He reached her door and knocked, announcing himself and putting on his best professional smile just before the door swung open. When he had first seen Ms. Kayo's photo, he had almost groaned out loud. She was beautiful, the type of beautiful that meant he would be fending off creepy touches and unwanted marriage proposals throughout the entire assignment. There was nothing quite as gross as having to physically remove sweaty fanboys from a venue. Up close, he could better appreciate just how beautiful she was. The black hair that had been in loose waves in her professional photos was now pulled back into a long braid, her skin was pale and so flawless it still seemed airbrushed in real life, and her eyes were purple. Not dark blue or grayish mauve, but a vivid violet that was almost surreal. She was wearing a white apron splashed with yellow sauce.

"You're here!" she said with a bright smile and too-perfect teeth. There was mischief in her eyes. "You're Masaru, right?"

"Yes, ma'am. I am Suzuki Masaru. It's nice to meet you."

"I'm going to call you Masaru."

Great. "All right. Would you like to go over the schedule for the expo?"

"Later. First you have to help me with this." She grabbed his hand in a surprisingly strong grip and dragged him away from the entrance to her suite and into a small kitchenette. It looked like a group of children had run through everywhere except where Ms. Kayo's camera was pointing. Masaru's eyes widened at the utter disconnect between the clean working station and the random pots, pans, and ingredients strewn about the rest of the suite. He had never met a client quite this messy and clean before. They had all always been one or the other.

"Did you bring your own pots and pans?" he asked, surveying the chaos.

"Yep. I always bring my own equipment. Other people's things just don't feel right, you know? Now taste this." She shoved a spoonful of what Masaru assumed was what had stained her apron into his face, giving him no choice but to open his mouth and taste it or get covered in it. Thankfully, it was pretty delicious; somehow sweet and savory. Her eyes sparkled when he told her as much.

Masaru watched her talk excitedly to the camera, showing her audience how she had set up her tiny work station before showing them how to make an easy pineapple and shrimp curry over rice. He refused to get on camera when she asked, choosing instead to observe her on-screen persona. It was pretty much exactly the same as when she had interacted with him, but with less mischief and more cutesy language.

When she was done recording, Ms. Kayo handed him a plate of the curry and rice and started practically bouncing in front of him, excitedly asking how it tasted. Masaru could hardly lie when he was practically inhaling it, so he told her it was delicious around a mouthful. "Good, then you can help me while I make preparations for tomorrow. I'm going to demonstrate how to cook for a small dinner party. Just a three-course meal in the stage kitchen they set up in the main ballroom. Leftovers are part of your contract!" The last sentence was said with a sly grin and a wink. Maybe this job wouldn't be so bad if he was going to be paid in money and delicious food the whole time.

KICHIRO OPENED HIS EYES to a bright blue sky. It was a truly wonderful sight and, honestly, he didn't feel he could ask for a better day to die. He couldn't really feel anything anymore, and while it was nice to no longer be in pain, he knew that meant he didn't have much time left.

Much blood left. A shadow fell over his eyelids; he hadn't realized he had closed them. Looking up once more took great effort, but he managed it and standing above him was . . . a fox. But, no. That wasn't right. He was pretty sure foxes weren't usually taller than horses.

It was terrifying, grotesque, even. It was the basic shape of a fox, but far larger. It had white fur with strange black markings that seemed to shift and flow like living things. Its teeth were as long as his thumbs, they caught the sunlight and gleamed from blackened gums. But Kichiro wasn't scared of the creature, he was already dying; and more concerning than its dangerous teeth or unnatural size, he was captivated by its beautiful eyes. Two pairs of them, one just a bit higher than the other, and a shade of violet unlike any other he had ever seen. He had nothing to compare it to. The color so different from anything he imagined could exist in this world. The fox suddenly tilted its head as if it were confused and narrowed its eyes, looked at him more closely.

Beautiful?

The voice sounded as if it was coming from several different voices, speaking as one. The voices were male and female, young and old. It took him a moment to realize that the words had been spoken not into the air, but into his very mind.

No one has ever thought that about me.

Well, they should, he thought, the world getting more and more distant with each passing moment.

What is your name, human?

Kichiro.

The voices in his head laughed. It was strangely comforting for all its scornful mirth. Good luck? Stabbed and robbed in an empty field?

Yeah, he could see the irony too.

The fox leaned toward him, four eyes narrowing in interest. What if I saved you? Would you take me home? Call me beautiful again?

Kichiro wasn't sure what kind of blood-loss-induced hallucination this was. But he didn't see a point in arguing against it.

Sure, he thought, as he finally faded from consciousness. The sound of dark laughter followed him down.

MASARU WOKE UP SWEATY and shaky. It took him a few moments of looking around in confusion before he remembered he was in his hotel room. Right—the expo—Kayo.

It had been a dream. Why had it felt so real?

Masaru had never been able to remember his dreams very well. They always slipped away like sand through a sieve once he opened his eyes; but this one lingered through his showering, dressing, and meeting with Kayo. The chef was just as excitable and bubbly at seven a.m. as she had been the afternoon before. Masaru did two checks of the ballroom where the stage-slash-kitchen was set up, trying his best not to disrupt the cameramen setting up to record. Then Kayo called him up to the stage to help her set up.

"Can you plug this in, please?" she asked, holding out an electrical cord attached to an induction burner—at least that's what he thought it was. Masaru had always been terrible at cooking.

"Sure," he replied, taking the cord and plugging it into the side of the big counter the hotel had somehow carried onto the ballroom stage. He looked up afterwards and frowned when he noticed something. "Wait, isn't that a stovetop? What do you need this for?" As the words left his mouth, he realized how completely unprofessional they were. How was her equipment any of his business unless it was trying to kill her?

Thankfully, Kayo didn't seem bothered. "Oh! That's a good question. I should answer it during my demonstration." She smiled at him, though her body was still turned toward where she was organizing her utensils the way she would need them. "I always set this up because gas burners like those can be inconsistent. This one can be adjusted to maintain a consistent heat. So, for example, if I just wanted to simmer something, I can adjust the heat here to ninety-five degrees Celsius," she said, pointing to where a dial was attached to the side of the burner, "It's much easier to control the heat like this."

Masaru supposed he shouldn't have been surprised—she was always so enthusiastic, but it was still gratifying to hear her be so serious and knowledgeable about something. On an unrelated note, he wondered if he should go and buy an induction burner to cook with at home.

When they were done setting up, Masaru got out of her way and just watched the show while keeping an eye out for anyone suspicious, obviously. Kayo started with a classic miso and vegetable soup, cutting paper-thin radish and carrot slices into flowers before adding them in. Then she made the main course: a simple ginger-pork over rice recipe that was "easy to make a lot of and share" according to her. By the time she was done, the whole ballroom smelled incredible. Finally, she made dessert: custard cream filled dorayaki that reminded Masaru of going to festivals with his mother as a child. He, along with most of the audience, was starving by the time the demonstration was over.

"So, what's wrong?" Kayo asked while they were taking a lunch break, eating some of her delicious pork together. He gave her a surprised look; he had thought he was behaving normally. It wasn't as if they had spent a lot of time together yet. Had that dream really shaken him up that much? "You've been weird since this morning."

"It's nothing. Please forgive me if I've been unprofessional."

She pouted. Eating in morose silence for a few long minutes until he couldn't take it any longer.

"It's nothing, really. I just had a weird dream last night is all."

She whirled back toward him, bright smile right back on her face. The brat. "Really? What was it about?"

He sighed, resigned. "I was sometime in the past, maybe the Edo period, and I met a fox."

"Aww! I love foxes. They are so cute." She cooed, "Was it, like, an Inari fox? Could it talk and stuff?"

"Yeah, I guess."

She nodded thoughtfully. "Maybe that means you'll have a good harvest?"

"I don't have any harvest."

"Well then, maybe we should buy you a plant." And then she just nodded to herself as if she had made a decision. Masaru began to prepare himself for the small potted plant he was sure he'd be receiving soon. Coming from anyone else, he figured he would be pretty upset by the invasion of his personal life, but, somehow, he thought it was all right if it was her.

Kayo continued to munch away happily, and Masaru began to wonder when he had dropped the "Ms." honorific from her name. Then there was a dorayaki being shoved into his face. She did that a lot, he had noticed, like a child that wanted you to pay attention to something they had made. He took a bite and tried not to moan at how good it was. Judging by Kayo's face though, he hadn't been completely successful.

"I saw you eyeing those earlier. Is dorayaki one of your favorite foods or something?"

"Not exactly. They just remind me of going to festivals as a kid. The custard cream ones were always my favorite. But why didn't you make red-bean paste ones, if you don't mind me asking? Those would be the most classic version."

"The custard cream ones are my favorite too!" Masaru could not imagine a more child-like expression than the way Kayo bounced in her seat and clapped her hands together excitedly.

Masaru tried to focus on his job, but he couldn't quite get the image of the fox's eyes out of his mind, even as he fell asleep that night.

KICHIRO CAME TO, WHICH was its own surprise, but what was more surprising was his mother kneeling beside him, a concerned look on her face.

“Oh, thank goodness!” she said when she noticed his open eyes. Tears of relief began to roll down her cheeks. “We were so scared.”

He tried to say, “I’m all right,” but found his throat too dry for speech, and began coughing instead. Suddenly, a cup of tea was being gently raised to his lips. His eyes slowly followed the soft-looking hand holding the cup to beautiful woman sitting on his other side. She was pale, a similar shade of white to the fox’s fur, with long black waves of hair. And then he met her eyes, her beautiful violet eyes. She smiled at him gently and prompted him to drink by nudging the brim of the cup against his lips. It was brewed perfectly, and it instantly soothed his parched throat; he drank the rest of it slowly as his mother instructed.

“What— what’s going on?”

His mother gave a quick glance to the strange woman before replying, “This young lady says she found you in a field, missing your pack and delirious from a stab wound.” She had to pause and collect herself for a moment. “She said you told her she was beautiful and that you would marry her.” Kichiro felt his eyes widen a bit at that. “Then she took you to a nearby cave and nursed you back to health before bringing you back here.”

He blinked and looked back over at the woman. Did she have a horse? She didn’t look nearly big enough to carry a grown man anywhere, let alone an unconscious one. His mother touched his sleeve to get his attention again. “She won’t give us her name. She said she wanted to talk to you first.” This last sentence was said with an obvious question behind it, but Kichiro had even less of a clue as to what was going on than she did.

“All right,” he said carefully. He turned toward the stranger again. “Thank you very much for saving me. What would you like to talk about?”

“Could we, maybe, talk alone?” she asked shyly, looking down at the tatami mats under her knees. Somehow, Kichiro didn’t think she was actually shy at all. His mother gave a knowing “Of course” and a searching look at his face before she left the room. When he looked back at his savior, her shy look had been replaced by a smug smirk.

"I'm glad you're finally awake." How long had he been— "Less than a week. It took a little longer than I thought it would to heal you." Had she just— "Yes, I can hear you. Just like I did before." Suddenly, it all came flooding back, the blue sky, the fox. He gaped at her.

"You're the . . ."

She nodded, still smirking. "Yes, what do you think of this form? I couldn't exactly carry you back to this village in my true form. Am I still beautiful though?"

"Of course. Yes." Then his brain caught up a bit to the conversation beforehand. "Marriage . . . ?"

"Well, yes, obviously. How else am I supposed to stay with you? You can't just invite random women to live in your house with you."

She had a point, and really, Kichiro didn't think he could do much better than a fox god as a wife. He didn't really have that many options to begin with.

"All right, that's good. So, what's your name?"

But she just shook her head at him. "I can't tell you that," she said. "I'd lose my power. You'll just have to give me one to use."

Kichiro stared at her again. Was that how it worked? Well, it wasn't as if he spent a lot of time with gods. He looked at her and thought about all of the names he had ever heard. None of them seemed grand enough for such a being. Eventually he said, "Sukichiyo."

It was her turn to look surprised. "Beloved . . . for a thousand generations?" she asked, mulling over the name and its meaning for a moment. Then she smiled and gave a single nod. "Then, you should promise to love me forever." He smiled back at her, forever suddenly didn't seem so long.

AGAIN, MASARU WOKE UP shaken. The second night in a row of strange dreams and he really wasn't sure what to make of this last one. Why did his weird fox-wife look so much like Kayo? They weren't exactly the same, and yet, he felt like they were. They both gave the same smug expressions when they got their way. He shook his head. Having dreams where you marry your clients' Edo-period look-alike had to be against some kind of rules of conduct.

That day when he met with Kayo it was even more awkward as he couldn't get the dreams out of his head and she continuously sent him concerned puppy-eyed looks every few minutes after he refused to tell her what was going on. He knew it wasn't all concern though, as she would also wring her hands together in frustration at being ignored. The day before had been relatively relaxed, as she had just done the one on-stage demonstration and then taken some audience questions. But day two was much busier. Masaru had to follow her to three back-to-back panels. The first one was interesting enough; she talked about her favorite cooking tools and recipes along with three other chefs. Two of whom owned restaurants in Tokyo. The second panel was less interesting, as Kayo and her two fellow panelists talked about monetizing their social media accounts. Masaru couldn't even remember anything that was said in that panel.

By the time Kayo was done with the last panel about cooking and performing for an international audience, Masaru was hungry and frustrated. His bleak mood was compounded by the fact that he had to eat lunch separately from Kayo as she was scheduled for a meet-and-greet lunch with fans who had paid for top-tier tickets to the expo. It didn't help at all that he was forced to eat food from the expo instead of something Kayo had made. He would admit, at this point, that he was being a bit spoiled by her constant cooking and bubbly chatter. He normally found people with so much energy to be annoying, but her excited smile and childish movements somehow put him at ease.

They finally met up again to do one last demonstration for the day. Kayo teamed up with another chef to show their audience how to make proper yakitori. Masaru found himself once again reaping the benefits of Kayo's demonstrations for dinner that night before going to bed. With his head on the pillow, he secretly hoped to see Sukichiyo again in his dreams.

SUKICHIYO HAD SETTLED WELL into Kichiro's little village, if not entirely comfortably. He supposed that a god would be used to a bit more luxury than he could offer her in his thirty-house village. Still, she seemed happy enough to be the most beautiful woman anyone around had ever seen. And it was certainly gratifying for him every time another man offered her land or wealth or power to leave Kichiro and become their wife or concubine, and she refused outright. She never even showed interest in anyone else. She was also an incredible cook; the first thing she had done after properly introducing herself to Kichiro's parents was cook a small feast for all four of them. She made wild boar grilled with vegetables, bean curd soup, and a savory fish pancake. The pancake was something that neither Kichiro nor his parents had ever seen or heard of, let alone tried. She was obviously accepted into the family very quickly. Kichiro's mother started making noises about grandchildren that very night.

Also, once Sukichiyo arrived, she started tending to their personal gardens. They suddenly had more than enough ginger, radishes, carrots, red beans, and persimmons, and began selling. The village's rice field had also been flourishing ever since she came to live with them. Her arrival was taken as a good omen by many in the village, especially the nosy older women. There were, however, a select few who were sure her unnatural eye color meant she would eventually bring doom. Kichiro chose to ignore them, spending the many months since their marriage with his beautiful, talented wife. Apparently, she was trying to figure out how to get them into a nicer home before having children. One that could actually keep them warm in the winter, and that had more than three rooms.

"There is no more space in your family home," she told him, annoyance clear in her voice. "And I know you won't want to leave your parents behind, but I am not sharing a room with our children. So, we will have to move." Kichiro had never known anything outside of this village and a few neighboring ones, so he trusted her, as the better traveled one, to find a new place to live and start a family.

One night, about five months into their marriage, Kichiro retired to his room after a long day of fishing, bringing back a collection of wildflowers for his wife. Except, when he got there it wasn't his wife, but a strange man in his bed. The man was staring out of the open rice-paper window, into the steadily pouring rain. He had jet-black hair, cut above his ears, which was strange. Every man Kichiro had ever met had had hair that went down to their shoulders at least, trying to emulate the upper class. Kichiro was about to ask him who he was and what he was doing in his room, when the man turned and Kichiro saw his eyes. He would recognize those violet eyes and that smug expression anywhere.

"S-Sukichiyo? Is that . . . you?"

"Welcome home," his voice was a bit deeper than normal, but somehow, Kichiro could still recognize the cadence from his wife's speech. Kichiro should probably have been used to surrealness of life with a god by then, but in all honesty, this was still shocking. Then Sukichiyo saw what he was holding. He jumped up and practically bounced over their bedding to get to him. "Wild flowers? Did you get these for me?" Before Kichiro could answer, Sukichiyo had snatched the flowers and buried his nose in them to take a deep breath. Kichiro was momentarily struck by how . . . cute it was. Sukichiyo always bounced around like an excited fox, but that was as a woman. Kichiro did not know what to do with this situation. Sukichiyo finally looked up from his flowers and realized that something was wrong.

"What?" he asked, quickly going from excited to annoyed as Kichiro had trouble answering him.

"Um, you look . . ." Oh no, how was he supposed to end that sentence without enduring the wrath of a god? Or worse, his wife. Who was now glaring at him.

"I look what? This form is just like my other one! What's wrong with it?" he demanded.

"Nothing!" Kichiro said quickly. "Nothing's wrong. You're perfect."

Sukichiyo still looked a bit suspicious, like he didn't quite believe him. Much worse than that though, was the little bit of sadness threatening to creep into his tight expression, mouth in a firm line, and flowers clenched in too-tight hands. Kichiro had almost forgotten for a moment, how fragile his immortal god could be. Kichiro straightened up, and, looking right into Sukichiyo's eyes, pulled him in for a kiss. He pulled away and smiled before saying, with his more usual confidence, "You're beautiful."

Sukichiyo's smile sprang right back onto his face, and Kichiro distantly resigned himself to living with this insanity for the rest of his life. He wasn't married to a woman, after all, he was married to a fox.

MASARU WOKE UP AND felt like he was having a heart attack. He was sure his dreams were getting weirder. He had definitely never dreamed of being married to a man before. That day, when he went to meet with Kayo, he felt off and uptight the whole time. It didn't help that, after doing one last panel, she was scheduled to do the dreaded autograph signings. There would be extra security there for all of the guests, but Masaru was still worried. He began to relax a little bit when they announced that the booths would shut down soon. Kayo had been smiling brightly and chatting happily with all of her fans, even seamlessly sidestepping a few of the more forward requests for dating or marriage that came her way. He had only had to glare at a handful of sweaty fanboys to get them to leave and let the next fan in. Only two people had asked her to sign their body pillows. So, all in all, it was shaping up to be a good day last day.

Then, as one of the last fans stepped up to the booth, he noticed Kayo's smile shift to something more strained. The man in front of her had sweat-soaked brown hair and was wearing a long green coat, also covered in sweat. Masaru approached cautiously at first, but when he saw her eyes change from worried to scared he immediately reached out and put a hand on the man's shoulder to get his attention. Masaru had barely processed the knife's existence before it slid between two of his ribs. Time slowed as bright pain bloomed from his chest. He stared into crazed, bloodshot eyes as he started to fall. The last thing he heard was Kayo calling his name.

THE DAY WAS CLEAR and warm again. The sky blue as the day they met. Sukichiyo walked beside him as Kichiro told her the story of how he and a friend had stolen an old woman's robes once and used them to convince another girl in the village that they were a Yama Uba, come down from that mountain to eat her. Sukichiyo laughed loudly and freely at his childhood antics before she suddenly turned and grabbed both his hands in hers.

"It has been almost a year since we met," she said, still smiling, but now there was a slightly nervous look in her eyes, and he could feel her hands clutching tightly at his own. Kichiro nodded along with her and waited for her to continue. Sukichiyo slowly brought a white peach from the small bag she had attached to her hip and offered it to him. "I grew this for you, as a gift," she explained. The peach was perfect, not a single bruise or cut or spot marked its skin—it looked ripe and delicious. Kichiro smiled and reached out his hand to take it, but something stopped him from touching it.

He wasn't sure what was wrong, but every time he tried to take the gift, he found himself unwilling to do so. He watched as his wife's smile slowly slipped, being overcome by the nervous expression.

"What's wrong?"

"Nothing. I'm just . . . not hungry." Well, that sounded ridiculous. He had never refused something she offered him, ever. Why couldn't he take the peach? What was wrong?

Sukichiyo just stood there in bewildered shock. Her hand holding the piece of fruit still stretched out toward him. Then he heard someone calling his name from further down the winding path they were walking on through a meadow near the rice fields. Kichiro was honestly so relieved to have a way out of the awkward conversation that he didn't hesitate to start toward the man calling to him. The man was from his village and was having trouble carrying a container of water back home. Kichiro reached him and realized he was one of the few men from his village who didn't like his wife, but he was hardly going to refuse to help him because of that. As soon as Kichiro knelt down to help lift the water, he heard Sukichiyo cry out.

"Kichiro!" He looked up, or he tried to, but couldn't move and blackness engulfed his consciousness once again.

MASARU WOKE UP SURROUNDED by whiteness. A hospital room. He tried to move his hand before he noticed the IV attached to it. That was probably why he wasn't in any pain from the knife wound he distinctly remembered getting. Oh no, his mother was going to freak out when he told her he was stabbed on the job. She had been having nightmares about him being an extra in American action movies since he started working as a bodyguard. When he looked beside his bed, Kayo was standing there.

"I'm pretty sure only family is supposed to come into the room," he pointed out.

She shrugged, unperturbed. "I told them I was your girlfriend." Oh, well, what were professional boundaries anyway? Then he noticed what she was holding. Cradled in both of her hands was a white peach. Unblemished and ripe. He stared at it.

"What . . . ? From my dream?"

"Seriously?" she asked, and when his eyes returned to her face he saw her pupils were now slits, the teeth in her smile were too sharp, and then the hands holding the peach were tipped with sharp claws.

"It was real?"

"Yes."

"How did it end?"

"You were stabbed. Again." And, yeah, she did look pretty mad about that. She offered him the peach again. "Eat it." He reached for it again, but couldn't. Her eyes began to water. "Why? Why won't you take it? Every time . . ." Every time? "Yes! Every time I find you again, you won't eat the peach, and then you die again, and for some reason you almost always end up being stabbed! Why do crazy people around you always have knives?"

Well, that was a lot to process at once, but most importantly, "Why do you keep trying to give it to me? What does the peach do?" he asked. Okay, maybe that wasn't the most important thing but . . .

She huffed and tossed the peach onto his bed before turning her back to him and folding her arms across her chest. "It's a special peach that I grew after we got married. It's supposed to make you immortal. So we can be together. Like you promised! But instead you just keep dying and—"

As she spoke, Masaru felt something like a bubble popping in his mind, like a barrier he hadn't known was there breaking down and dissolving. Kayo's words were cut off abruptly as Masaru picked up the peach and took a big bite of it. The crunching sound made her turn around to see Masaru happily munching on the peach.

"This is really good," he said around a mouthful. She gaped at him. "Maybe it was, like, a consent thing? Have you ever told me what it did before?" He looked up at her. "Are you crying?"

"Shut up!" Yep, that was definitely a sob there. He got up, distantly realizing that he had just eaten a peach of immortality and probably didn't even have a stab wound anymore. Yeah, maybe life-changing decisions shouldn't exactly be made while on morphine, but he would have plenty of time to unpack that later. Actually, he had forever. He walked up and gently touched Kayo's shoulder.

"Did you think you needed to trick me into staying with you?" he asked, voice soft. She just wiped her eyes, back to looking human again. "What's your name?" he wondered, remembering the . . . memories he'd been having. "Can you still not tell me?"

She buried her face in his chest and mumbled “Sukichiyo.”

“What? But I thought that was—”

“I was a wandering god,” she explained. “I didn’t have a name, or a place.” The “until you gave them to me” was left unsaid. And as Masaru gave her the first kiss of forever, hc couldn’t help but feel that Kichiro had been a good name—he actually felt pretty lucky.

Vieques

Kathrine B. Dixon

I OPENED MY EYES TO FAINT CLACKING SOUNDS. NOT MORE THAN SIX INCHES from the tip of my nose, a yellow crab waved its claws in the air. It stared at me, or at least vaguely in my direction, with those creepy sideways bug eyes and stood on tiptoe, frozen in mid-flight like I'd just caught it climbing out of a second-story window with my jewelry. I blinked, and in that brief moment of absolution the little guy ran like the devil.

"Whoa, did you see that?" I whispered hoarsely to Neil. It was no use. He was fast asleep on his stomach, snoring, face buried in his beach towel.

This was just the sort of encounter I'd wanted to come here for. I'd read about the snorkeling, and the 300-year-old Ceiba tree, and the wild horses. I'd read about the midnight tours of the world's brightest bioluminescent bay, where you could rattle microscopic organisms with a wave of your hand and they'd leave a trail of aquamarine light behind you in the water like you're some kind of fucking sun god. I'd read that that bay was dying, just like me, and I wanted to see it before we were both forgotten forever.

I'm pretty sure Neil came here to drink. In the three years we'd been together, I'd learned well enough that that's what you do in his circle. You put in seventy hours a week at the office and every night at the bar; on the weekend you're "seen" and you let people see you. Every so often you can escape to a beach in the Caribbean or Mexico or

Florida and get drunk for a week straight, to recharge so that you can do it all over again. Vieques is not a destination that any of Neil's friends have stories about, but it's cheap and relatively easy to get to, and everything in our lives seemed to be changing so fast anyway, so he'd agreed.

Before I met Neil, I'd never taken a real beach vacation in my life. The vacations I'd taken as a kid consisted mainly of pilgrimages to historic homes, battlefields, museums, even cemeteries—a strict diet of educational experiences. It turns out old habits are hard to break. In my research before we left home, I'd learned that all of Vieques is a battlefield of sorts. I'd read about how since before World War II the island had served as a testing ground for the US Navy. The military had dropped bombs over nearly two-thirds of the island up until about ten years ago, when a bomb had gotten too close and killed a civilian and the overwhelming public uproar had finally driven them out. They'd left their mess behind them under the auspices of a wildlife refuge and, where it got really messy, a Superfund site. As a result of this mess, it was claimed that the Viequenses suffered a 26 percent higher cancer rate than their neighbors on the mainland. I decided not to share this last fact with my mother.

Once we got here we'd figured out pretty quickly that we were staying on the wrong side of the island. Vieques has precious little nightlife to speak of, but what nightlife there is, is in Esperanza, on the south side of the island. In fact, everything worth seeing—or, at least, everything noted on the map we picked up when we arrived—is on the south side of the island. We had made arrangements to stay at a bed and breakfast on the north side, in Isabel Segunda. (I say "we," but it was really Neil—my condition determined enough of our regular daily lives, so I'd decided to leave the specifics of the vacation planning to him.) Isabel Segunda is the administrative center of the island, which is just about as fun as it sounds. On top of that, when we checked in the proprietor of the hotel casually mentioned that the chef at our place, supposedly a Beard award winner and the main reason Neil wanted to stay there in the first place, had decided to take the week off with no warning, turning our luxurious bed and breakfast into a "bed and fend for yourself." What's more, we (there's that "we" again) had elected to ignore the guidebook's advice to rent a jeep to get around, and by the time we got here and realized our mistake there were no more jeeps to be had on the whole island.

But, we'd made the best of it. Our hotel had an infinity pool, and we'd found a decent beach and a little dive bar with a cutesy Spanglish name both within walking distance, so for a while we were all set. The bar sat right on the northern coastline and had a view of a shipwreck in the azure water of the Atlantic and no customers except for us and a handful of "regulars," escapees from the Lower 48 living out their Caribbean fantasy existence. On our second day on the island, we'd sat there for an obscenely long afternoon, drinking cane sugar Cokes (Neil's with a generous pour of Don Q and a lime wedge), chatting and petting the dogs that padded about the establishment, probably in violation of some kind of health code if anyone gives a damn about codes around here. One of the regulars had claimed to be a chef at a restaurant in Lake Geneva, not far from where we live. It occurred to me that maybe she could step in to fill the void at our bed and breakfast, although I didn't suggest it. And then at some point in the afternoon she disappeared—her buddy showed up, and they went for a drive and, it was understood, to smoke some weed. (I could have shared some of my legal stuff, I guess, but that would have started an awkward conversation and put a damper on things.)

Other than the time we'd spent at the bar, for nearly the entirety of the past three days Neil and I had been arranged side by side on this same nondescript stretch of sand, alternately either face down or face up in the sun, occasionally wading out into the water to cool off, like fat touristy sea lions sunbathing on a rock. Give Neil an IV of rum and Coke and he's happy as a drunken clam, but if I'm being honest I'd been pretending not to be antsy since we got here. I wanted to explore.

Neil had no interest in exploring. I can't say I blame him, really.

He'd been having plenty of new experiences at home, between the doctors and the specialists and the tests and the experimental treatment options and all the hard things that no one in his family had ever had to deal with before. He hadn't signed up for this. And, judging by the fact that he seemed to be drinking even more heavily than usual, I suspect he'd been wrestling with the question of whether he could even do this thing at all anymore. Right now, asleep in the sun, he was probably dreaming of freedom and relief and guilt. If he'd been brave enough to mention his concerns to me, we probably could have talked it out. I would have tried not to take it personally. As it is, he's been pretty stone-faced, like he's determined to tough everything out without any help and without acknowledging any weaknesses. Him alone, and me alone, and us alone together. If only he realized it could be so much easier if it were us together, together. But that's something he would have to come to on his own. You can't force people to understand the things they only want to pay lip service to.

No, if I was going to have any fun here, I was going to have to leave Neil to his beach towel and his private tragedies. So, on the morning of the fourth day of our vacation, I asked the proprietor of our hotel to call me a cab. As far as I can tell, the cab system on Vieques is basically just locals with cars willing to make some extra money by shuttling the tourists around (the ones who had ignored the guidebook advice to rent a jeep, that is). Our hotelier called one of her friends, Alejandro, and I told him where I wanted to go. He was chatty. He asked how long I was staying and what I'd seen so far, and I was too embarrassed to tell him that I hadn't even been to the south side of the island yet, so I told him I'd just arrived the night before. Normally I would have resisted any sort of attempt at conversation with a stranger, but I was in a strange land and the atmosphere here made me feel looser, like a different person altogether. And I was having an adventure.

A few minutes later I saw what I'd been keeping an eye out for, and I told Alejandro he could let me out, which he did, wishing me a pleasant rest of my stay (everyone seems to be well trained in hospitality here). Three days ago, on the cab ride from the tiny Antonio Rivera Rodriguez Airport to our hotel we'd passed this line of scooters glinting in the sun, and I had dismissed a thought before it was even fully formed. This kind of thing wasn't for Neil and me—more specifically, it wasn't for me. These were for those other people, the ones who said yes to everything. I was not one of those people.

I was surprised at the nonchalance with which the girl behind the counter handed me a helmet and keys. I had to resist the urge to ask if she was sure she wanted to do that. But then she motioned for me to follow her outside, and together we walked around what for the next couple of days was to be my scooter, assessing it for any damage. After a quick once-over, she nodded and told me I was all set. Little did she know how not "all set" I was. I tried to act self-assured, like I wasn't a gringa out of my depth, like I wasn't convinced the scooter would fall over while I was trying to mount it and the girl would have a bunch of new nicks and scratches to mark down on her little paper there. I was relieved when she walked back inside—I'd assumed she would want to stay and watch, and maybe point and laugh.

I strapped on the helmet, feeling like an even bigger idiot, and to my great amusement I managed to swing my leg over the side of the scooter with no mishaps. I turned the key in the ignition and talked myself one more time through the steps the girl had shown me (there were basically two: twist and squeeze). I took a few laps around the parking lot. Soon, I was zooming with very little control up the hill that led out to the main road. As I was wondering whose bright idea it was to build a scooter rental establishment on the side of a hill, I was passed by a semi truck going down said hill at sixty miles an hour, and the noise and gust of air washing over my fragile, exposed human body made me gasp and lose my train of thought. I had to remind myself to keep my eyes open. Yet, I was still upright, and I was moving in the right direction, and that's much better than I expected at this point. Once I felt comfortable enough to loosen my grip on the handles, I might have cracked a smile. When I reached a straightaway, with no cars or trucks around, I even ventured to feel a little bit badass (as badass as one can feel on a scooter, that is).

This was the beginning of the rest of my vacation, but I didn't know where to start. My map was in my backpack, and I'd been so preoccupied with just taking these first steps—finding the place and getting my feet under me—that I hadn't actually planned out where I would go once I got the means. Quite possibly I believed I'd end up in a ditch before I could get very far anyway. But now that I was speeding along with the island opening up in front of me, my only impulse was to go where no one else would be.

So, whenever I got to a juncture, if the other cars around me on the road turned right, I turned left. I kept doing that until there were no other cars on the road. Slowly, the landscape around me began to transform. The open plains that had stretched for miles on either side of me gradually began to close in, until I found myself riding along under a lush green canopy. The air was heavy and fragrant. I navigated new twists and turns, praying at every bend that I wouldn't come face to face with a car that had inadvertently crossed over into my lane (as the drivers here seemed wont to do). Occasional breaks in the canopy revealed the working farms where families laboring outdoors paid no attention to my scooter buzzing by. The only signs of any kind were the kilometer markers counting down, I imagined, to some extraordinary event.

At the 7.0 kilometer mark exactly, I stopped. Or, rather, I was stopped, by a hermit crab in the middle of the road. I got off my scooter and knelt down to get a better look at the thing, motionless on the asphalt, trying to make itself look small, its little red, spiny legs drawn up but still clearly visible inside a perfect piebald shell. I was tempted to just pick it up and move it over to the grass and have done with it, but I couldn't bring myself to exert that kind of domination. Instead, I made encouraging sounds, hoping to convince the crab that it was okay to unfurl itself, that everything would be better, it would see. Nothing happened—my words must not have gotten through to its tiny ears or, if they had, this guy wasn't buying it (and after all, what reason did he have to trust me?). So, for a long time I was just quiet. If I was quiet enough, I thought, the crab would figure I'd left and he might feel comfortable enough to skitter away to safety. But none of those things happened. As long as I sat there, he did too. He had seemingly resigned himself to becoming roadkill. It reminded me of Neil.

When I looked up again, the weather had changed. I'd read that storms could pop up unexpectedly in this tropical climate, and now the sky—a brilliant, cloudless blue when I'd left the bed and breakfast this morning—had grown overcast. In quick succession, I felt a single drop of rain on my bare arm, and then another, and a few more. Apprehension set in. The half-hearted tutorial I'd received at the scooter rental place hadn't instilled much confidence that I could handle wheels on wet pavement. Fortunately, just across the road from where I'd been communing with the hermit crab, I noticed an unmarked path and a tiny dirt parking lot no bigger than a postage stamp. I decided to leave my scooter there to wait out whatever storm might come.

Once my scooter was safely parked, the question became what to do with myself. There weren't many options—I could either stand still or move forward. So, with my backpack on my back and my helmet slung over one arm, I started to clamber down the rocky path that stretched in front of me. It looked like a creek bed of some sort. There were shallow pools every few feet. Ripples blossomed in these pools as a steady stream of raindrops dripped into them from the low-hanging bushes and tree branches. I didn't know where this path would lead or whether I'd be able to maintain my footing on the steep and slippery terrain, but I just put one foot in front of the other and eventually emerged to discover that I was standing, once again, on a beach. Go figure.

This beach wasn't like the one where Neil and I had stopped speaking, however. It was narrower and rockier and wholly deserted. And, if my eyes didn't deceive me, the sand looked to be much darker, almost black. In fact, it was black. This must be the Playa Negra, the black sand beach I'd read about, the one that even locals supposedly didn't know existed. What my guidebook had not said was how, in the rain (which was falling even faster now), this narrow strip of land became beautiful and cruel, a vengeful goddess of octopus ink. Do not venture here, she warned. This is not for you. I stepped out onto the sand anyway. It felt like walking on the surface of the moon.

My clothes and shoes were soaked, and a strong wind whipped salt and sand and the ends of my hair across my cheeks. The octopus ink goddess was clearly trying to show me just how big a mistake I'd made. Pressing forward, I wound my way gingerly around the next bend, and from its crest I caught a glimpse of four large shadows, maybe thirty feet away across a narrow inlet. The rain obscured the finer details of these alien creatures, but I could tell they were marching in a line, nose to tail, and that they were moving in my direction. It was a band of horses, making a beeline right for where I stood.

Earlier in the day, I'd spied some of the island's free-roaming horses, but it had been from a safe distance, on my scooter. I'd never been this close to something so large and unpredictable in the wild, and now I was about to be outnumbered by large and unpredictable things. Panicked, I ducked into a small clearing surrounded by bushes. I hoped I would remain obscured from view when they passed, but honestly I had no idea if this was the right thing to do. What if it was exactly the wrong thing? What if I startled them and they turned on me, what if they reared up and charged? I started to choke on the rain and on my own hair. I couldn't breathe. I realized, helplessly, that I wasn't prepared. I tried to remember what I'd read, but my desperate lizard brain was coming up empty. I was alone out here at the ends of the earth. If I didn't come back, Neil would have no idea where to look (and I considered the very real possibility that he might not even try). I also noticed, for the first time, the water filling in my footprints on the beach behind me. If the worst happened, my only avenue of escape would be out into the waves that now crashed ominously against the dark sand.

In this moment of truth, I was humbled. I had to admit that I'd avoided beach vacations all my life not because I didn't see the point in them, but out of a deep terror of the ocean and the unknowns lurking in its depths. Even when I'd been able to talk myself into wading out in the surf these past few days, every little piece of seaweed became a jellyfish or a shark surfacing to wreak havoc with my limbs. The octopus ink goddess sensed that fear and fed on it; what's more, she had sent for reinforcements. She wanted to crush me. What I wouldn't give for a shell to curl up in, like that hermit crab with his illusions of safety.

As I waited for my fate to be decided, it occurred to me: I knew something that octopus ink goddess didn't know. I knew how little I had to lose, and how much I had already risked. I knew the burden of fear and uncertainty I was capable of shouldering, one person alone. And I knew, definitively, that I'd rather be trampled to death by wild horses on a solitary black sand beach or even swept out to sea by a vicious current than waste away in a hospice bed any day. (I'd be willing to bet the locals would say the same.)

I was loaded for bear when the horses ambled slowly by, so close I could have reached out and stroked their salty hides. When they passed without so much as a curious glance, I was relieved, and more than a little deflated. But who was I kidding, to think that my very presence would disrupt their onward march? After all, I was just another visitor.

Conversations with a Monster

Karla Young

THE GIRL WOKE IN THE LEAN-TO SHE'D BUILT FROM POKEWEED AND BRANCHES left behind when her father pruned the trees. She curled into the coarse warm fur of the dog pressed beside her and thanked her earlier self for the tarp and blanket she'd used as a floor. Above her the sun found its way through weave of the roof, blue sky like pieces of stained glass from the windows at church.

She sensed someone watching, not threatening, but definitely there. Rolling over, she peeked through a gap in the back wall and saw a person, or animal, she wasn't sure. It was tall, like a giant, and furry.

"Hi. Who are you?"

The creature startled as if to run, then stopped.

"You can see me." A statement, not a question.

"Of course. And you can understand me."

"Of course."

They pondered each other for a moment. The creature braved comment next.

"You are not afraid of me."

"Why should I be? You're not scary."

The creature chuckled at that. Chuckled, like a person.

"I'm big and hairy, a monster. How is that not scary?"

"You're bright magenta. Magentas aren't scary."

The creature laughed outright. "I am not sure what's most shocking—that you see me as magenta or that you can see me at all."

"Well you are Magenta." She gestured to the dog. "Today he is Lime. And I am Shamrock. Don't you agree?"

"Indeed, I do." The creature brushed a hand across its face, considering. "May I come closer to sit with you where we can converse? I would like to hear more about your colors."

"Sure! Most people laugh when I talk color. They think I'm making it up. Honestly, I think they're kind of stupid. I mean, the colors are there whether they can see them or not."

Folding its legs, the creature settled outside her tent. Massive, there was no way it would fit inside.

"By what name should I call you?" it asked.

"My name is Cricket. Actually, my name is Sara Ann but everyone calls me Cricket. I guess because I'm small. And I talk a lot. What's yours?"

"I'm Granville. And this valiant beast beside you?"

"He's Bear. I named him when I was two. My mom thinks it's because he's bristly and black or because I didn't know many words then, but it's really because he is a bear."

Granville smiled. "Yes, that one surely has the spirit of a bear. How old are you, Cricket?"

"I'm seven, which is why I'm only seven trees back. See?" She pointed to the line of trees between the lean-to and her home, which sat in a clearing just outside the woods. "You can count them—seven. That's as far as I can go by myself while I'm still seven, so I can see my house and my mom can see me. And I have to take Bear with me so he can keep me safe."

"Your mom is wise." Granville nodded.

"How old are you, Granville?"

"I am much older than you can count."

"Are you a boy or a girl?"

"My kind do not have boys or girls. We are both and neither."

Her eyes opened wide. "Really? How do you have babies? I know where babies come from." Cricket was proud she knew about making babies, unlike her friends at school. When she'd told them at recess last spring, they called her crazy, just like with the colors. The teachers knew she was right but told her not to talk about it anymore.

Granville explained, "We make babies a different way, but we do not make them very often. Because we live many years, we plan carefully and create rarely."

She nodded. Somehow that answer made perfect sense. "I don't want to hurt your feelings . . . Do you mind if I ask what you are? Are you a person?"

"Your questions do not hurt me, Cricket. I have been called by many names, none of them accurate. I am not human, but I am a person. We call ourselves the sentinels. Do you know what a sentinel is?"

She shook her head.

"A sentinel is someone who watches, like a guard."

"What do you guard?"

"That is a difficult question. Mostly precious creatures like you."

That answer also made sense. "You're like Bear, for when I go into the forest."

"Yes, very much like that. I believe your mother wants you now. You must go."

Cricket turned to see her mother walking across the yard. Bear gave a short "woof."

"She shouldn't see you. I'm not supposed to talk to strangers."

"She cannot see me."

"Like the colors."

"Yes. Like the colors."

"Okay. Will you come again?"

Granville nodded yes.

"Good. I like you, Granville."

"I like you too, Cricket. Now take Bear and go."

The girl smiled, stepped out of the lean-to, and ran toward home.

The mother watched the girl look up and run toward her, admired the strength of her daughter's thin legs, her wavy dark hair in its usual tangle. The child resembled neither her mother nor her father in appearance but was clearly their child in personality, equal parts responsible like her mother and spitfire like her father.

She took Cricket's hand. "Let's get you and Bear some lunch."

Watching from the kitchen window, the mother had seen the girl talking to open air, one hand twisted in Bear's rich fur and the other gesturing. She chuckled again remembering. That girl could befriend a mayfly, or a wasp. She was happy to have the girl find friends where she could. Goodness knows, this far up the cove, there weren't many children to play with.

She settled Cricket at the table with a sandwich, gave Bear his bowl, and returned to the dishes in the sink. She inhaled the familiar smell of basil and rosemary rising from the pots warming on the sill, paused to watch the dust motes floating on the rays of sun.

THAT AFTERNOON, CRICKET returned to the lean-to and waited. When Granville did not appear, she talked to the trees. She wasn't sure if the trees understood, but she liked to pretend they could, rustling their leaves in response. She'd seen her mother do the same with the cat, alternating comments about the weather with meows.

When the trees fell silent, she listened instead to the birds. They sang to each other and sometimes called out in joy or alarm. She named them by their sounds. "Tat-tat-tat-tat-tat" was the woodpecker of course. "Twee-wee-wee-wee" was the one her dad called a junco. Her favorites were "twoo-oowee-oowee" and "wee-uh-uh." She watched, hoping to see one as it sang so she could match the sounds to its shape.

Ever patient, Bear rested beside her, raising his head only once when deer, a doe and a fawn, passed.

Cricket decided that, if Granville returned tomorrow, she would ask about the trees.

Granville nodded. "Yes, of course the trees understand you. They do not know your words, but they listen and recognize the essence of what you mean."

"Do they talk back to me with their leaves?"

"No, the sound of the leaves in the wind is just that, but the trees do talk. They talk to each other and talk about you. They like you."

Cricket was pleased. "Can I learn to hear them?"

"Hearing trees is possible but difficult. They talk underground through their roots and fungi in the soil. You would have to bury yourself in the ground to hear. Even then, you would not hear words as you think of them. Still, there are some who can hear.

"The key is to be still, close your eyes, and open your mind. Then see what ideas appear. In some cases, those ideas are the tree. If you think of water, perhaps that is the tree thirsty or predicting rain. If you think of babies, perhaps it is the tree talking of its saplings."

"That's weird." Cricket laughed. "I don't believe it."

"Weird like you as Plum instead of Shamrock today?"

Cricket laughed harder. "Yes, exactly. Weird just like that."

AS THE SUMMER PROGRESSED, Cricket's mother needed help in the garden during the mornings, so Cricket could only visit the lean-to in the afternoons when she conversed with Granville on many topics, not all of them weird.

Cricket talked about her school friends and the animals she loved. She showed Granville her 120-count crayons and what she thought were her best pictures. Granville talked about his travels and what it felt like to be furry in summer—not hot, actually. Sentinels were good at keeping cool, and warm in the winter. Granville visited many places and preferred mountain forests where few people lived.

"Don't you like people?" Cricket held her breath waiting for the answer. She wondered how much Granville liked her. She hoped it was a lot. She had started to feel about Granville like she felt about Bear, her heart getting squeezy and excited-feeling when the sentinel appeared.

"I like you, Cricket, very much."

Cricket smiled and twined her hands together in front of her face.

Granville went on, "You and I spend time together and have become friends. When I encounter most people, they do not want to be my friend. Either they run away and never admit what they have seen, or they chase me with cameras to prove that monsters exist."

"But you're not a monster."

"They do not know that." Granville sat up straighter, arms wide open. "Do I not look like a monster?"

"Maybe they think you'll eat their dogs."

Laughing, Granville asked, "Why would I eat their dogs?"

"I just figured people in the forest would have dogs and, other than themselves, they'd be worried about their dogs."

"Ahh, of course. Yes, I am sure some people are worried about their dogs." Granville paused, searching for an explanation she could understand. "People see what they expect to see and that becomes their reality."

"So . . . if I see you, and expect you to be a monster, you will be?"

"To you, yes."

"When we first met, if I thought you were a monster, would you have eaten Bear?"

Granville laughed, delighted with her innocence. "No, but you may have run away assuming I would eat Bear, and that would be your truth."

"But you'd never really eat Bear."

"No."

"Okay, good."

CRICKET MISSED GRANVILLE when it rained. One such day, she sat at the table where she could see the woods and sharpened her crayons. One after another she peeled the paper wrapper, then twisted the crayon in the plastic hole on the back of the box. She colored many animals and birds, so the browns, blacks, and grays were dull along with the greens for the trees and grass. The others she used for color circles. She was careful never to peel the paper so far that she lost the names. At school they only had two blues, light and dark. At home, she had many—Cerulean, Cornflower, Aquamarine, Denim, and Periwinkle, which she thought was more of a purple but came in the box with the blues.

She heard a knock on the door and turned to watch as her mother answered.

The mail. "Hey, Jasper."

"Lynnette." The mailman nodded up, a slight lift of his head. "Got a certified letter for you. Have to sign for it." Her mother flipped the screen hook and opened the door to let him in.

Cricket watched her mother wipe her wet hands on her hips, take the pen, and sign.

"It's from the mines. Everyone up and down the cove's getting one. Can't be good."

"Nope, can't say I'm glad to see you today."

"I reckon not."

Her mother closed the door, set the letter down unopened, and picked up the phone. "Cricket, run upstairs to your room and read for a bit."

Through the open door to her room, Cricket heard her mother speaking and knew her dad must have answered at work. "David, what you heard in town? It's happening. We just got the letter."

Later that night, Cricket listened as her parents argued in their room next to hers. Bear crawled into her bed and Cricket buried her face in his side. Her parents seldom raised their voices even when she disobeyed.

"You've seen what they do to the people who refuse to sell. They buy the land all around them and leave them surrounded by scald."

"Exactly. That's precisely why we can't sign. Every one of us who does leaves the rest of us exposed."

"The Tates and Russells have already agreed."

"So?" Her mother's voice was thick, crying. "What about the Lamberts, Warrens, and Slaughters? They'd never sell."

"Not the older ones but their kids have been bugging them to move to town for years. They're saying maybe it's time to get out. The prices are fair."

"Fair? Fair to who? To the mining company peckerwoods? To us? To mountains?"

Their voices dropped. Cricket could barely hear her father. "I'll call everyone in the morning. And James Bryant. If we do this, we do it together and we're going to need a lawyer. It's going to cost, maybe everything."

"I know. Everything's all we've got."

The wall between began the soft rhythmic shake it made late at night when she was supposed to be asleep. She looked out the window, looking for the moon or maybe the shadow of a monster. With Granville as her guard, everything would be okay.

The mother worked the garden alone the next morning, needing time to think without Cricket's chatter. The girl was happy to have a full day in the lean-to. Lynnette thought of her own summers in these mountains. Both she and David had grown up here before leaving for college and their first real jobs.

When pregnant with Cricket, who was still Sara Ann, they'd decided to return to the cove, wanting the same kind of childhood for their daughter with freedom of space and knowledge of their roots. Now the damn mining company wanted to blast it all away.

She paused leaning on her hoe. Through blurred eyes, she saw Cricket lying on her back, arms and legs straight in the air. Was she playing dead bug? Or just checking their length as Lynnette remembered doing herself as a child. Who knew with that child and her imagination. Did every parent look at their child with this kind of wonder? Lynnette hoped so.

IN LATE SUMMER, CRICKET'S routine of gardening and Granville took on a new aspect with evenings centered around visitors gathering in her family's kitchen to discuss mining company offers, strategy, and law.

Cricket tried to follow their discussions but eventually stopped listening. She knew they were trying to save the mountain and couldn't agree on how. She didn't like to hear them argue and taught herself to tune out the sound and focus only on the color. When they argued the adults' colors got bigger and swirled with each other. Her father's usual clear Red turned muddy when it mixed with Mrs. Lambert's Brown. Mr. Bryant remained steadfastly Navy Blue. Her mother, whose own color was Crystal when they were home alone, became a rainbow, mixing all those around her.

When Cricket felt her own Shamrock darken each night, she went to bed, leaving Bear behind at the top of the stairs.

"I think I should tell my mom about you."

"Perhaps. That is for you to decide."

"Do you think she would believe me?"

"Probably not. Would you believe you?"

"Probably not."

Granville clarified, "Why do you want to tell your mom about me?"

"My parents and our neighbors are upset about the mining company and the mountain. I figured if they knew you were here, they would know everything was okay because you protect it."

Granville paused. "I cannot protect your mountain, Cricket."

"But you said you were a guard and you're here on the mountain."

"I said I was a sentinel. My job is to watch, which is something like a guard. My ability to take action in the world is limited. Have you noticed that, despite my size, I rarely leave footprints where I walk?"

Cricket nodded.

"For me to leave a print, I must exert extraordinary effort. I rarely do this because it is not my role. I am here to experience your world, not change it. I can be here, but I cannot stop the mining."

"Well, you're not a very good guard then." Cricket felt her anger in her stomach. She left the lean-to early and returned to the house. Bear followed.

The adults in the kitchen that night didn't argue. Cricket listened as they reviewed the plan. None would agree to sell. The mining company already owned the top of the mountain, but they would not get the cove. James Bryant would file for a legal injunction to halt mining, pending an environmental impact study. To Cricket's ears the solution sounded simple. She wasn't sure why they'd needed so many nights to decide.

LYNNETTE HEARD THE BLAST mid-morning, the boom ricocheting from one side of the cove to the other. Her first thought was for Cricket, who stood outside her lean-to, looking to the sky. Then she dialed David. "They're starting. Before the injunction, they're already blasting."

"Dammit to hell. Call James. I'm on my way. Call everyone. Get them to the top of the mountain."

GRANVILLE HAD APPEARED just before the boom.

"Cricket, you need to come with me."

"Where are we going?"

"To the top of the mountain."

Then the blast, followed by a moment of startled silence. The birds took flight with raucous cries. Cricket stood and followed the birds with her eyes.

"Look at me, Cricket. They are destroying the mountain. Only you can stop this."

"Me?"

"Yes. You. Your parents' plan will not work alone. They need your help."

Cricket felt peevish. Her remaining anger churned. "Why me? You're huge and you can't do it. What makes you think I can?"

"Because you are Cricket. The girl who sees colors and attempts to talk to trees."

That made sense to the girl. She nodded. Another blast.

"Okay, but I need to tell my mom if I'm going beyond the seventh tree."

"There is no time. I'll tell your mom. We have to go now."

Cricket took a deep breath. "What about Bear?"

"He will stay here."

"Okay."

Cricket stepped out of the lean-to and took Granville's hand. She felt the scratchy heat of her friend's chest as the sentinel tucked her in tight.

LYNNETTE QUICKLY COMPLETED her calls. She heard David's truck and went to the back door to call her daughter. Cricket was gone.

David came in the front. "Get Cricket. Let's go."

Suddenly Lynnette knew. Her face dropped in terror.

"She's already on the mountain."

"Holy hell. Let's go."

Cricket's father drove with force that sent gravel spinning at each curve of the road. He passed neighbors also on their way up. His daughter near those blasts. He felt gray like the color he saw in his wife's face.

TO CRICKET, THE TRIP THROUGH the forest felt like a whoosh. She sensed Granville's legs move, running, but without touching the ground. In the space of five breaths, they stood on the ridge, facing the mountain crest, already partially blown open into piles of upended trees and shattered rock. A yellow backhoe loaded with debris turned and moved toward Cricket and Granville.

The backhoe driver startled when he saw Cricket, a small girl with unruly dark hair standing where moments before had been open space. He did not see the massive creature, standing behind her in the brief feet before the nearly vertical drop to the creek bed below.

Hitting the brakes, the driver dialed his foreman. “Uh, Boss? There’s a girl up here.” Granville could have laughed at the shock on his face.

“You gotta be kiddin’ me. Well get her out of there. You see any parents? Probably some tree-huggers making trouble.”

“Um . . . there’s no one else here. “

“A little girl by herself on top of Black’s Mountain. Today.”

“Yep.”

“Aw, shit. I’m coming.”

Cricket watched the man in the machine talking on his phone. She saw him turn from Tan to Gray and knew that he was unhappy, like her dad when he paid the bills.

Granville reassured her. “You’re doing great. I am right here with you.”

The man in the machine looked at Cricket and they waited. Cricket could hear the rustle return to the trees. Other workers walked over and stood beside the backhoe waiting to see what the foreman would do.

“Talk to them, Cricket.”

“About what?”

“Just talk. Ask them what they are doing. Ask them questions like you ask me.”

Cricket nodded. “What are you doing to the mountain?”

The foreman walked up as she began. “What’d she say?”

Cricket repeated, louder, “What are you doing to the mountain?”

“We’re mining it for coal.”

“Why?”

“Because people need coal to power electricity to keep their homes warm and to turn on the lights.”

“Why do you need to blow up the mountain to get the coal?”

"Because it's too expensive to do any other way."

Cricket nodded. That answer made sense. "How do you get the coal after you blow everything up?"

Not sure why he was answering, the foreman responded. "Well, if you would get out of the way, we could push this rock out over the side and then we could dig out the coal."

"But the creek's down there and the trees."

The man shrugged. "Uh. Yeah."

"And the animals and birds."

"Yeah. They'll hear it coming and run away."

"Where will they go?"

"I don't know. They'll find new homes." The man huffed in frustration. "Look, we need to get back to work. Get out of the way, girl." He separated himself from the group of gathered workers and walked toward Cricket.

Cricket felt Granville's hand tighten on her shoulder. "I have you, Cricket."

She met the foreman's eyes. "No. This isn't your mountain. I'm not moving so you can push it into the creek."

He grabbed Cricket on her arm, squeezing hard. Cricket could feel it would bruise. "Come on, girl. Let's go."

Reassured by Granville's gentle hands, firm on her shoulders, Cricket planted her feet to resist the foreman's pull and raised her chin in defiance. "No."

The watching miners turned as they heard the crunch of vehicles on the gravel. Cricket's and the foreman's eyes remained locked on each other.

"Get your hands off my daughter." Lynnette jumped from the truck. Her heart went cold at the sight of the foreman, her daughter, and the drop-off behind. A small scuffle and Cricket could go over.

"It's okay, Mom. I've got this." Cricket drew herself up as tall as she could and jerked her arm out of the foreman's hold. She saw his color go dark, almost laughed when she realized he was scared. Of her.

David looked at the stare-down between the grizzly man and his daughter and held Lynnette back. “Hang on. This is exactly the delay we need.”

“What the hell, David? Are you saying we should leave our seven-year-old daughter between the edge of the mountain and that?” She gestured to the gathering collection of workers in hard hats and a newly arrived mining company executive, incongruously dressed in a suit and muck boots.

“Yes. Look at her.” Unexpectedly, he chuckled. “She’s a force to be reckoned with.”

Cricket’s small body radiated determination, her jaw clenched and the sun shining from behind through that wild mane of hair.

Another truck came into the clearing and James Bryant jumped out, paperwork in hand. “Stop all work. I have a signed injunction.”

“Damn it to hell!” The mining exec turned to the crew. “Clear out.” To James he said, “You know this won’t stick. We’ll be back in a month.”

“Maybe so, maybe not.” His face split with a grin. “That little girl over there would say not.”

At that Lynnette sprinted to Cricket and pulled her away from the ridge.

On her knees, both crying and angry. “What were you thinking? How did you even get up here?”

Cricket answered simply, “I was the only one who could save the mountain. Because of the colors. Granville brought me.”

“Child, most of the time I have no idea what to make of you but dear God I love you.”

“I know, Mama. I love you too.”

Anger fading, Lynnette cried, pressing Cricket’s head into her shoulder. Her daughter, this little Cricket, so small and so strong.

Cricket twisted to the side just far enough to see Granville nod a smile and whoosh away.

GRANVILLE HELD HER HAND later at the lean-to. "After today I will not see you for some time."

"Yes, I know."

Granville wasn't sure why she continued to surprise.

"Keep Bear close to you. Your mother and father as well. They love you very much."

Cricket nodded.

"The animals and trees of the forest. They know you are special and not to be harmed. You can trust them. Be more careful with the people. What endears you to the creatures of the forest is what frightens people who are not ready for you.

"You are more powerful than you know. For the first time in a long while, I have hope for this world. I am proud of you, Cricket."

They sat together in silence.

"May I hug you, Granville?"

"Yes, of course."

Cricket wrapped her arms around her friend, at least as far as they could go. "I'm proud of you too, Granville. You did more than watch. You took me up the mountain."

"Yes, I suppose I did."

Loathe to let her go, Granville held her a moment longer, then another. "I must go now. The other sentinels have heard what is happening here and are gathering to discuss."

Cricket perked up. "Will you tell them that extraordinary effort is worth it?"

"I will." Granville smiled. "I absolutely will. I am going to tell them that watching and protecting are good. But sometimes we have to do more.

"Remember the mountain, Cricket. Do not be afraid to step out and be who you are. Do what you must when the time is right."

Cricket nodded and they sat in silence until the sun began to settle behind the mountain.

"I love you, Granville."

"I love you too, Cricket."

And with that her friend was gone. Cricket rested in the lean-to, eventually falling asleep. When she heard her mother call her in for the night, she stepped out of the lean-to, then stopped with a smile.

To the side of the seventh tree, Cricket saw one massive footprint in the soft earth. She bent over to inspect it, then took off her own shoe and pushed it into the forest floor, leaving her small print next to the large one.

"Travel safe, Granville."

Softly in the breeze, she thought she heard the words "I do."

Contributors

Daniel Zeiders was born in Annapolis, Maryland, but hasn't been back since he was a toddler. He went to high school in Bartlesville, Oklahoma, and worked at the movie theater. He liked to sit in the projection room and watch the giant spools of film turn and turn. Daniel Zeiders received a BA in English from Oklahoma State University and an MFA from Minnesota State University. He currently lives in Texas above a family of armadillos.

Ry Molloy lives in Las Vegas, where he waits tables on the strip. He has another piece forthcoming in *Not Your Mother's Breast Milk*. Follow him on Instagram @Power.Twink.

Alexander Abbas Kayhani was born in Portland, Oregon, in an Iranian-American household. In university, he studied philosophy with a focus in identity formulation and philosophy of science. He has been writing poetry since 2013 and fiction since 2016. Currently, he lives in New York City and performs at various open-mic nights. Follow him on Instagram @whistling.hawk.

Anne Katata is a writer and a food and culture consultant. She has a BA in English literature and an MA in architecture, and she has worked as an architect and project manager in the US and Europe. She lives in Los Angeles, California, and Vilanova i la Geltru, Spain, with her husband and a family of cats.

Dawn Marie Martin grew up in the Pacific Northwest. She attended Seattle Pacific University and worked in the utility industry most of her career. She has ten siblings and became a mother at the age of seventeen. Her childhood was filled with instability, financial hardships, and a strict religious rule. She is proof you can overcome your childhood circumstances and follow your own path. She is currently working on a memoir.

Carter Keeling is an environmental consultant working in the San Francisco Bay Area. Living in a politically active and artistically enriching community of the Bay Area, Carter has observed the power that local-minded writing can have on the world at large. Carter is interested in how human loves intersect with the natural world—their mutual and exclusive joys, fears, and threats. He is currently completing his first chapbook of poetry.

Heather Hein lives in Colorado and works with individuals with disabilities. Her hobbies include hiking, camping, teaching yoga, and helping women have babies in her spare time. She is a member of Northern Colorado Writers, Scribophile, and the Lighthouse Writer's Workshop. She has a degree in human development and family studies from Colorado State University and has worked as a newspaper editor. She lives with her two children, two dogs, and husband, who has been her muse for the last twenty-eight years. She is currently working on her first novel.

Mary E. Monte grew up in West Chester, Pennsylvania, and has been writing since she was old enough to hold a pencil. She loves writing poetry as well as creative nonfiction. Currently, she is earning her master's in industrial and organizational psychology and working. In addition to writing, Mary enjoys plants, cooking, reading, and exploring new places.

D.S. WALDMAN is a writer, painter, and wanderer based in the foothills of the Los Padres National Forest. He holds a BA from Middlebury College and will be enrolling in the MFA program at San Diego State University this fall.

Though **PATSY LALLY** currently lives in Portland, Oregon, she grew up in Brooklyn. She was born to a Southern mother and an Italian father. It was not, however, a home of magnolias and spaghetti. It was a joyless house without respite from violence, chaos, and fear. Nancy Drew saved her life as the first protagonist who offered her the magic carpet of books to transport her out. Books became her hiding place and refuge. For beer and pretzel money, she is an international tour guide. She is currently working on a novel, *Broken Angel*, wherein a twelve-year-old girl is committed to saving the life of the newborn baby brought into the house. It takes place in Brooklyn, 1956. Her stories always deal with the effects of childhood trauma on the adult survivor.

ARIEN REED, a transman and 2019 MFA graduate from National University, lives with his husband and is a staff member at Fresno City College.

SARAH ANN COHEN is an optimistic undergraduate studying literature at the University of California, San Diego. When she has the rare break between essays, she enjoys writing as much poetry as humanly possible and forever looks to other poets to improve her skills.

CASEY GIBSON is a Los Angeles resident born and raised. She recently graduated from the University of Southern California with an undergraduate degree in narrative studies. She writes primarily fantasy and science fiction and is generally trying to be funny, whether or not she is successful is open for interpretation. When she isn't writing or getting her life in order, she often makes desserts in her family's kitchen, contributing to the American consumption of sugar.

Kathrine B. Dixon, who used to refer to herself as a recovering lawyer, is thrilled finally to feel comfortable just calling herself a writer. Originally hailing from Illinois, Kathrine recently drove an RV from Chicago with her boyfriend Daniel and their three cats (Smokey, Elphie, and Beezil) to relocate to Portland, Oregon, where they are enjoying a plum tree, a grapevine, and wide-open skies.

Karla Young has an MA in literature and planned to teach at the college level before opting for a less scintillating (if more lucrative) career at a large technology company. Having returned to her first love, Karla writes stories and novels that question the perceived boundaries of human experience. She lives in an old farmhouse in central Kentucky with her husband and small herd of animals and kids, who help keep her priorities in order and ensure the kitchen is never clean.

www.ingramcontent.com/pod-product-compliance
Lightning Source LLC
LaVergne TN
LVHW081324110826
845149LV00007B/1592

* 9 7 8 0 9 9 7 7 9 4 4 8 9 *